THE BRIDE

Millie Yundi

Contents

My boyfriend has been cheating on me with my sister for two years.

"We looked at each other and then lmy sister laughed.

- Merry Christmas, sis! Mila said happily in the arms of my boyfriend.

They grined at me on my bed, completely naked.

- Screw you, Mila.

I walked out of the room and slamed the door."

That was my Christmas' present two years ago.

The solution?

Leave.

Away.

Far away from everyone.

Maybe even forever.

Out of sight, out of mind!

Chapter 1

2 years later

"Alma, Jayna", my secretary called as she walked into my office.

"What's the matter?" I mumbled, immersed in my work.

"Your mother is on the line."

"Tell her I don't work here anymore," I answered without looking up from my work.

"She's been persisting since this morning. Answer it," she replied. "I'll transfer the call to you."

I sigh, leaning back in my chair. The phone on my table rings. I hesitate to answer. My cell phone has already been ringing all weekend and I haven't bothered to answer it. Honestly, I don't feel any worse. The door to my office opens and Jayna gives me a falsely surprised look.

"Answer," she orders, standing in front of me.

I look at her blankly before getting back to my work. She approaches my desk before picking up the phone and handing it to me. I glare at her and she walks out of the room with her tongue out. I hang up and the phone starts ringing again.

Dear Lord.

"I'm sorry I hung up, I didn't mean to take your call," I say as I pick up the phone.

"How ungrateful," my mother says.

"Hi, Mom. It's always so nice to hear from you."

"Of course, it is. Hello," she grumbles. "Alma, you have to come home in two months."

"May I know why?" I wasn't planning on setting foot in Spain for a while.

"Your sister has a big announcement to make. To the whole family." My mother says.

"If it's about her wedding, count me out. Take me off the family registry if you can. And tell people I'm dead. It's better for both of us." I say reading my notes.

"Don't be ridiculous," she grumbles. "Your grandmother would also like to see you again. Be there on the fifteenth of the month."

She hangs up on me without letting me argue. She always has to involve my grandmother in the story when I reject her. That old hag. I still have two months left before I have to leave.

I go back to work with my mind elsewhere. The clock on my desk shows 6:00 pm. My last sketch is finally finished. Tomorrow is a day off. I will finally be able to relax.

Shortly after I arrived in New York, I was hired at Dynasty. One of the biggest luxury brands worldwide. Shortly after I arrived, the company decided to specialize in weddings and events. There were hiring for wedding planners, stylists, jewelers as well as cobblers and estheticians.

After winning a competition and several interviews, I was hired as a wedding dress designer. I am in charge of designing the ideal outfit for the brides-to-be in which they will say "YES". Despite the pressure on my shoulders, I became the head designer. Now, I only create dresses for the most important customers.

I open the door to my condo and head straight to my room. I put my bag on my desk and collapse on my bed. Fatigue takes over and my eyes close.

The buzz of my phone wakes me up from my nap. I answer straight away without looking.

"Hey, Alma! I need you to come somewhere with me!" My best friends Meavy shouts. "Meavy? Let me sleep. I need to sleep", I emphasized. "Please."

This is my best friend, Meavy. A bundle of joy that I met while I was in New York three years ago. At the time, I was just celebrating my graduation and we ran into each other at a bar. Since then, we have been unseparable. She even came to study in London two months later so we could stay together.

"Only if you listen to me until the end. Do you remember the nightclub that was supposed to open in Las Vegas? It's going to open tonight at midnight. The owner is a close friend of mine. I have two cards for the VIP room", she sings on the other end of the phone.

I sit down on my bed abruptly, which makes me dizzy. "I'm coming."

"I knew it! In an hour, at your place. Be ready. Love you."

I hang up and get out of bed to get ready. I go into the bathroom to take a nice hot bath and shower. I get out and stand in front of my wardrobe, looking for clothes to wear.

I hear the front door open and the sound of heels walking towards my room. My door swings open and Meavy enters the room.

"Holà, before you say anything, I came with more news. The club is hyper-selective and very trendy. Only rich people will be there, so the dress code tonight is: chic and sexy."

"Thanks a lot, Meavy. Can you go out now?"

"Not yet," she says as she approaches me.

She unties my robe and looks at my underwear.

"Still a big fan of lingerie, I see," she says, making me blush.

I slap her hands before closing my robe. She laughs as usual. Meavy opens my huge dressing room and helps me to choose an outfit. I put on my dress, a watch and a pendant.

"What shoes?"

"My black Prada suede wedge sandals. At the bottom on the right of the shoe storage." Meavy approaches me and hands me my shoes. I thank her before putting them on quickly. I put on a black coat and grab a golden clutch. We finally leave my room."The private jet is waiting for us at the airport. We'll be there by midnight for the opening."

My best friend grabs me by the arm and we walk out of my house. We get into her car and she starts the car. The ride goes by in a flash and we get back in a car that Meavy rented in advance. I turn on the radio and one of our favorite songs is being played. We start singing at the top of our lungs the whole way. Meavy parks in front of the nightclub."Mila is getting married to James," I say quickly.

" She- What? I thought it was just a one-night stand."

"Apparently they were much more serious. I have to go back to Spain in two months."

"Do you want me to come with you?" Meavy offers, taking me in her arms.

"So you can ruin their wedding and have it all fall on me? No, I'll be fine. Don't worry about it." "Then get out of the car! Come on," she said, pulling me by the arm. "We came to have fun. We're going to have a drink and forget all our problems tonight. We're in Vegas! Vamos, chica!" Meavy shouts in the street.

I get out of the car laughing with Meavy. The nightclub looks like one of those places so fancy that no one dares to enter. What attracts the attention is mostly the queue that goes to the end of the street. About a hundred people are waiting for the opening.

Meavy moves forward and gives me my VIP card. She slides it on a reader stuck on the wall. The door opens and I do the same before slipping it into the pocket with my phone.

The heat in the room hits us full force. A smell of perfumes mixed with sweat floats in the air. The music is deafening and the bodies of the people on the dance floor are swaying to the rhythm of the music.

Meavy goes on the dance floor dragging me with her. After a few minutes, I go to the bar to have a drink. The barman serves me a glass of vodka. I continue to order all the cocktails of the bar, just to forget that my sister is going to get married to the one I thought was the man of my life.

Chapter 2

My head, gosh. I feel like it's going to explode. I open my eyes and the light blinds me briefly. I meet a foreign face in front of mine. It certainly isn't Meavy. She is not so hairy - not at all, in fact. A scream escapes my mouth and I grab the sheets to hide my naked body as I move away from the man.

"Stop screaming so early in the morning," the man next to me says.

On closer inspection, I'm not home. My heart is racing in my chest as I try to figure out what's going on. I feel like my heart is going to give out on me at any moment. Maybe I overdid it yesterday.

"Who are you?" I asked as I backed away.

"You don't remember," The man said, straightening up. "Maybe this will trigger your memory." He raises his left hand in front of me and I see a wedding ring. I twist it around his finger before I see my initials engraved on it. What the hell ?

"This can't be happening", I whispered. "What did I do?"

"You made me marry you", the man said. "Last night."

Is this a joke? It has to be.

A nervous laughs escapes my lips. He smiles and lies back down. Now that I see it more clearly, this man isn't bad at all. He is rather young, probably in his twenties. He has a handsome face and light blue eyes that bring out his jet-black hair. Not to mention his muscles.

"Are you enjoying the view?" He asks playfully.

I snap out of my haze to look him in the eye. I had to get caught. He could pretend he hadn't seen me checking him.

"What happened yesterday?" I asked more seriously.

"You came into the room I booked and sat down next to me. You took a few drinks in a row. Then I offered to pay you a cab home."

The more he talks about it the more I remember.

I walked into a room thinking it was the exit to the roof after climbing all those stairs. This man was there with other people. They were all talking to each other until I got there. He was incredibly attractive in his three-piece suit. I sat astride him without paying attention to the others.

"You're beautiful," I whispered, putting my hands on his cheeks. Much more attractive than James. So much more. . .

A tear rolled down my cheek without me realizing it. He wipes it away quietly.

"Is everything alright?" he asks after a moment.

"Do you need me?" I asked without thinking.

"I don't know that yet. But you definitely need to sober up," he said, lifting me up and walking out of the room.

"Marry me."

"I'll call you a cab before the space cake I ate starts to kick in." He ignores me and goes outside of the room.

I shake my head and pass him a piece of cake. Meavy's famous mushroom cake. He gobbled it down thanking me before heading down to the bar. We had a drink together and then... . The space cake started to kick in. He was in his own world.

I walked to the wedding hall and dragged him with me. He pouted the whole way before he realized where we were.

"What are we doing here?" he asks at a loss.

"We are getting married?" I asked again. "Please."

"No! I am a free man!" He shouts, turning around. "Or maybe a woman?"

"A human," I said, laughing stupidly. "Help me find someone else then."

We went inside and somehow went to register our marriage and pronounced our vows. None of us really knew what we were doing.

I have vague memories of coming here and then nothing.

"This is the last time I'll ever take drugs. In my whole life", he announces. "I thought I was in a dream until I woke up at 4 a.m. and found you asleep on my bed. I wish it had been the effect of the mushrooms and the weed."

"But you remember everything," I said.

"I don't remember a thing. We just taped us going to the city hall and coming here. It brought back some memories to watch the tapes, that's it."

A silence settles between us.

"I think we slept together," he says with a frown. "It's the most logical explanation of our nudity." He lifts the sheet and looks underneath. I do the same and see a brown stain on the sheets. We really did it. Besides, he should change the mattress.

"I gave my virginity to a stranger," I muttered in shock.

"You weren't the only one that was a virgin," he retorts with a sigh.

"I want a divorce," I said abruptly. "Now, right now."

He burst out laughing and look at me.

"I don't think that's going to be feasible."

"Give me one good reason why not."

"Plus, we signed a contract that there would be no divorce between us. We'll be together until death do us part," he concluded with a sorry smile.

What was I thinking signing that? My 'husband' pulls out his phone and shows me the famous contract with my signature at the bottom and our smiling faces next to the contract. I have a vague memory of thinking that just like that, he wouldn't abandon me.

We look sober. And my hair and make-up still look good.

No more drinking for the next ten years.

"It's illegal," I countered.

"I guess so. Go tell that to my folks. I don't know how the officiant found this document. I was sure I burned it. It's already too late, we got a marriage license. And I don't think any of us can afford a divorce. The contract mentions five hundred millions of dollars."

"It can't be true. Why would the officer let us get married when we were so wasted ?"

A nervous laughs escapes the man in front of me. He shots me a glare that could kill me on the spot.

"Because of you." " Me ?" "Yes, you. He said 'no' and you took out 3 000 $ in cash from your purse telling him to sign. He didn't even wait for you to talk before signing."

Money really makes people go crazy.

"Can I see the contract ?"

"Here."

I read the document several time while my heart is about to give out. I can't afford to spend that much on a divorce. Well, I can but I don't want to. My savings would diseapear right this instant.I might as well face the consequences of my actions as a responsible adult. Even more so because I was the one who asked this man to marry me. And I vividly remember taking him all the way to City Hall when he told me he was very well single. It seems that we are connected, for life.

Or at least until my saving fund can drop that much without me going broke."Can you remind me of your name? "I asked, defeated.

"Gabrielo Moretti," he replied, holding out his hand with a smile.

"Alma. Since we both can't afford a divorce, let's do our best to make this marriage work, Gabo. We don't really have a choice at this point. "

"You can count on me."

He is about to continue when my phone rings.

Incoming call: Mom

"Mom, this is really not the right time."

"Not my problem. The announcement has been moved up by two months. Try to find a date by then."

"All right. Have a good day, Mom."

Oh, my, what an old hag... I'm dropping on the mattress. I'll have to ask Gabrielo to come with me. I can't risk people knowing I brought a date when I'm married. I learnt the hard way that lies don't stay hidden long. What did I do to deserve this?

"Was that your mother? You look like crap," he points out curiously.

"As always, when she bothers to remind me that she's alive," I replied.

I get up from the bed, pulling the sheets behind me. I head to the bathroom to do my toilet quickly. Except that I'm not at home and I don't know where things are stored.

"Gabrielo," I called through the bathroom.

"What can I do for you, Alma?" he asked as he entered in his birthday suit.

I turn around abruptly and look away. I understand where my aches and pains come from now.

"Could you get me a toothbrush, toothpaste and a towel and soap, please?"

Gabo pulls everything out of several cupboards and sets it down by the sink.

"Make yourself at home", he says, leaning against the door frame. "I mean, you are home technically."

"Would you mind going outside? I would like to shower."

"You have nothing to hide from me anymore, Stellina.""Stellina?" I repeted, frowning."It's Italian," he explains, stroking my hair. "A lovely word to describe my lovely wife."

What is he talking about ? We've only known each other for a few hours and he's already that confortable ?I don't even know what to think anymore."Close the door when you shower", he adds as he leaves.I finish showering and get out, wrapped in the towel Gabrielo gave me. He is sitting on the bed wearing a tuxedo talking on the phone. He sees me and points to a dress on the bed. I hear a voice shouting from the other end of the phone.After thanking him, I go back into the bathroom to change. He even put on underwear. It's embarrassing, but I don't have much choice. I dress quickly and go out after putting on my shoes from yesterday."Are you okay," I ask as I saw him sigh."Everything's fine," Gabo says, looking at me. "My mother just found out that I got married."

Chapter 3

"Are you planning to go see your mother?"A nervous laugh escaped me. I already don't get along with my own family. The proof, the only call my mother has made to me in two years was yesterday. Look at the fallout. On top of that, I just found out that I got married. And that I was no longer a virgin. I think that's enough to handle in one morning."No, I told her to wait and we'll see her later. For now, I have work to do. I'll drop you off at your place.""I don't live in Vegas," I replied.

"We're in New York. I'm sorry but I opened your purse to look at you ID, you are from here, right?"

"Yes, I am. I live near downtown", I replied, shaking my head. "How did we get here?""Private jet," he replied, taking my hand. "You fell asleep just before we embarked and woke up when we arrived."We leave his apartment by the elevator. We arrive directly in a parking lot loaded with cars. Gabrielo stops in front of a huge black car. The kind of car whose price must have seven or eight zeros in a row. I sit down gently on the seat after Gabrielo opens the door for me."Where should I drop you off?" Gabrielo asks."In front of the Time Warner Center, please."

"Not at your place?"

"No, I have to go see someone first."After a fifteen minutes drive, Gabrielo drops me in front of the mall before starting again to go to work. I take out my cell phone from my bag and call Meavy. After the second ring, she answers the phone.

"I know you're back in New York, I saw your post. Meet me at Magnolia Bakery, right now."

I hang up without another word. Twenty minutes later, Meavy comes trotting in on her heels.

"All right! I'm here," she huffs as she sits down.

"Meav', why did you let me you leave to go drink on my own last night?""Correction: you went out for a drink and had a sudden urge to go to the toilet. I offered to go with you and you said you were fine. I waited for a while, but you never came back. I looked for you for a good 30 minutes before I gave up. So what happened?" She asks while drinking her coffee.I raise my left hand in front of her so she can see properly. Meavy chokes on her coffee before regaining her composure. She grabs my hand and moves it back and forth to observe the ring on my ring finger.

"You got engaged without telling me. And my invite? Where is it ?"

"Married. I got married," I repeated, glaring at her. "Because last night, someone wanted to let me drown my sorrows in alcohol."

Meavy avoids my gaze and fiddles with her cup. She gets up abruptly and sits down next to me on the bench.

She blinks several times and kisses me on the cheek. "I'm sorry. I didn't know something like that would happen."

"Meavy, what am I going to do?"

"Divorce", she proposes. "Why stay together ?"

I explain to her what Gabrielo explained to me less than an hour ago. She bursts out laughing and starts shaking me. I glare at her without saying anything.

"Why would you sign this kind of paper voluntarily? What's gotten into your head? Stop dreaming when you're awake, for God's sake !"

Ah. . I was expecting it, Meavy's frankness. Always so painful yet effective. She sighs before finishing her coffee.

"If you needed a date I would have crossdressed with a gorgeous wig and be perfect for you ! You know that, right ?"

"I know that." Way too much. "Meavy do you know how screwed I am ?"

"I know. I'm gonna murder him and make it look like an accident."

"I'm not going to prison. Let's just get on with our shopping day."

The last Saturday of the month is usually the only shopping day Meavy and I are allowed. The reasons are simple, we want to rest on the other weekends. And especially because we need money to pay the bills and eat before that. Well... We decided to slow down with our shopping, and spend it all on the last weekend of the month.

"Alma, I haven't asked you yet, but what is your so-called husband like?" Meavy asks at the exit of a store.

"6'4. Black hair, blue eyes and the whitest smile I've ever seen. He is cute."

"Let's hope he's just a normal cute guy that you met in a club and not a creepy stalker that waited for you to get wasted", she concludes.

"Stop it, I just slept with him. What if i caught an STD? Or if I was pregnant ?"

"You used a condom, right? Alma ?"

"I don't know. I think so but I'm not sure."

"I guess you're going to see the doctor next."

"Meavy !"

"What ? One of us needs to be freaking out while the other thinks for the both of us. I need to stay calm if I want to think things through."

Our shopping day ends quietly and I call a cab to go home. Now that I think about it, I don't have Gabrielo's number. But it's not that bad. Maybe we'll never cross paths again.

I finally arrive home and put all my bags in the hall. My phone rings in my bag. The screen shows: Gabrielo. When did I give him my number?"Hello?"

"Hey. Where are you right now?"

"I'm at my place. Do you need something?" I asked.

"Can you send me the address, please", he asks. "I wanna talk to you about something."

I do what he asked before quickly putting my new clothes away. I start to cook after having showered and the doorbell rings. Gabrielo is on my doorstep waiting. I open the door and he starts to smile.

"Am I disturbing you?" he asks, running a hand through his hair.

"Not at all, come in. I was just making dinner."

I leave the kitchen and join Gabrielo in the living room.

"I wanted to talk to you," he begins, turning to me. "My whole family knows I got married. So I want you opinion on the matter. Do we keep this whole thing secret or not ? "

"Let's keep it between us. Not secret. I mean we're already married. I said I want to make things work. Just give us time. I can't move have a secret relationship with someone I barely know nor get official. "

Plus I litteraly don't know if you're a creepy guy that's sitting in my living room.

"Great," he said, exhaling sharply. "We should grab a coffee sometime soon. Or-"

A stomach rumbling cuts him the word. Gabrielo looks away, blushing. He looks cute when he blushes.

"I think we'd better eat before we make any decisions. There is nothing pressing after all."

"I think so too," agrees Gabrielo.

The dinner passed in a good mood between our laughs and each one telling his day. It had been a long time since I had gotten along with a guy so well. Maybe this marriage will go smoothly.

Time will tell.

Gabrielo still seems to have some work to do and some calls to make. I should get started too. I take out the sketches from the day before to work on them. I have to finish making a wedding dress before the end of next month. Not to mention the adjustements that'll need to go with it.

"Finally, finished!" I exclaimed as I stretched.

I look at the sofa and see Gabrielo sleeping peacefully. It's already 10:30 pm. Has it been that long? At least I was finally able to finish the sketches and determine the fabrics and gems we will use.

"Gabrielo? Wake up."

I shake him by the shoulder and he grunts, moving his head slightly. I repeat my action and this time Gabrielo grabs me by the waist. He holds me firmly in his arms and continues to sleep. Well, I could stay like this for a while before waking him up.

Since we are face to face, I have a good view of his face. He is ruthlessly handsome. I grab him by the jaw before caressing his cheek. He opens his eyes still asleep. He rubs his eyes before looking at me, totally lost.

"Sorry", he says, releasing me.

"That's okay. Instead of sleeping on a couch, you'd better sleep on a bed. You'll end up with aches and pains."

"Are you inviting me to sleep here?" He asks, grabbing my waist and pulling me closer.

Chapter 4

"Hum," I smile, "since we're married, anything is possible. I just want to get to know you better first. Sleeping with a stranger bothers me. Don't take it personally."

"I'm joking," Gabrielo says, getting up. "I know you're not like that, Alma."

Wow. That was creepy. Like really creepy.

"What do you mean by that?" I asked, totally lost.

"We've already met before. That's why when you proposed to me, I said 'yes'. Did you really think I would marry a stranger overnight?"

I did.

"When was that?"

"You remember that, Stellina. For now, good night," he says as he leaves my house.

Did I know him from before? What is he talking about? I'm sure if I'd known a man this handsome in the past, I'd remember him. Unless we never spoke. Either way, I have no idea.

It's all a little too disturbing for me. But I would not mind getting an answer to my question. Anyway, I'd better go to bed for now. The ringing of my phone cuts short my thoughts and I pause to answer.

I answer when I see Gabrielo's picture on the screen. When did this happened ?

"Hello, Gabrielo? What's up?"

"Nothing important", he answers quickly. "I just wanted to tell you that my mother wants to meet you on Monday for lunch."

"What?! What do you mean, nothing important? That's super important !"

"Relax, she just wants to see you. You don't have to make a big deal out of it."

"I didn't prepare anything for this. Gabrielo! Why didn't you tell me before?"

"I forgot. Then we'll go to have lunch with her on Monday ," he concludes. "I have to go, I have an important call to take."

He hangs up and I start to panic. I need a gift and an outfit. Something original and unique for a good gift. Even though I have an idea in mind, it might be complicated to pull off. I take out my phone to make a call.

"Meav' I need your help, I say quickly through my phone".

"Breathe and tell me what's going on."

"My mother-in-law ! I'm meeting her this Monday for the first time. I thought I would have a little more time but I don't. I need a present to give her, an outfit and-"

"Alma!" Meavy interrupts. "Relax, if it's about an outfit, I'll come and help you. You need to have an idea for the gift and if there's one thing I've learned from my sister's experiences it's to be yourself no matter what. It will always be better than pretending. I'll come see you in the morning, okay?"

"Okay, I'm going to go take a bath and go to bed then. Good night."

Meavy hangs up and I collapse on the couch. I would never drink again in my life. I was able to forget my problems for thirty seconds only to have twice as many problems fall on my head.

In 48 hours, I went from single-which-sister-stole-her-fiance to married-woman-who-is-going-to-meet-her-mother-in-law. I hope everything goes well, especially because of this damn contract I signed. What kind of sane person gets married and signs up to never get divorced? Not to mention the little clause that said no adultery would be allowed under penalty of fine and lawsuit.

What kind of family did I end up in?

DING! DONG! DING! DONG!

The ringing of my phone together with the doorbell rings in unison in a deafening din. I turn off my phone without looking to see who is calling me before I go to open the door.

"Meavy I got it," I shouted as I opened the door.

"Finally, I've been waiting for five minutes," she said as she entered. "Now tell me everything."

"Before I tell you anything, I'm going to clean myself and get dressed. Then we'll see. If you want, I have your favorite coffee, the one that costs a bunch of money for nothing, in the cupboard."

Meavy rushes to the kitchen. I go to get ready and twenty minutes later I am finally dressed and clean. My dear friend is on my couch watching an episode of The Bachelor, like every morning.

"How much time is left?" I asked as I sat down next to her.

"It's over," she said as the credits rolled. "So, we have to choose an appropriate outfit to go see your mother-in-law. Wear something that looks very... You. Something classy and elegant. Keep it simple."

"Okay. I'll give it a try. Let's go to the dressing room."

After half an hour of searching, I finally found what to wear. Meavy plays my mother and criticizes everything she sees without chewing her words. Total Meavy. Now that I know what I'm going to wear, I just have to prepare a gift.

"Where are you going?"

"To prepare a gift?" I answer hesitantly.

"No, no, no. Not at all. When you want to be presentable, physically, it's all about the details. Fortunately for us, you work out to stay in shape. We'll prepare a manicure, a pedicure and a proper hairstyle. I'll think about the makeup later. And what perfume you will wear."

Meavy and aesthetics. Just thinking about it makes me cringe. It's not for nothing that she is one of the greatest image consultants in the country. I can always count on her in this kind of situation. But I think I spoke too quickly when I told Gabrielo to come this afternoon. It's already 11:30 and we haven't even done half of the things we need to do.

After I finally find the right hairstyle and accessories to match my outfit, someone rings the doorbell. Meavy goes to answer it and I put my indoor clothes back on. Now that I think about it, I'm getting really hungry. I haven't eaten anything since this morning and thinking on top of that doesn't really help.

"Alma!" Meavy calls as she comes into the dressing room. "I'm coming with your husband."

Damn! I had forgotten that he had to come here. And I'm still in my pyjamas, even if it's more of a mini-short and a very long t-shirt. Meavy enters the room followed by Gabrielo wearing suit and a tie. This guy really has no regular clothes ?

"He's a hottie, honey. Honestly, you did the right thing by signing this contract," Meavy whispers in my ear.

It's true she's always been the type to want to end up with a cute boy no matter what.

"I see you have company," Gabrielo says, smiling at me.

"My best friend, Meavy. Meavy, this is my husband, Gabrielo."

They smile at each other and Gabrielo turns to me.

"I just wanted to tell you that I will pick you up tomorrow around noon. Send the address of your company so I can pick you up. And about my offer yesterday, we'll discuss it when you're free. Is that okay?"

"No problem," I replied with a smile.

"Very well," he said, approaching me. "See you tomorrow, Stellina. Send me a message later."

He places a kiss on my cheek and waves to Meavy as he leaves.

"Wow, what was that?" my best friend asks, pulling me out of my thoughts. "I don't think I've ever seen you act so stupid in all the time I've known you. Could it be love at first sight?"

"Stop talking nonsense, Meavy! It's just that... It's nothing ! How about a manicure?"

" I'd love to!"

Chapter 5

Today is Monday. And who says Monday, says work. In a good mood if possible. I finally finished the sketches of the bridal outfits for the coming season. All I have to do now is get the brides-to-be approval.

Ah, marriage. I thought I would end up getting married after finding love and celebrating my twenty-fifth birthday. At just twenty-three, I am already married and with a complete stranger. As they say, love after marriage. Things often work out for the better in these cases.

We are going to have an important meeting with the president. I completely forgot what he wanted to talk to us about today. The annual meeting has already taken place, if I'm not mistaken. Unless it's today. I'm having trouble remembering. So much is going on in this company.

Dynasty is divided into four major departments which are divided into branches. As for the Wedding & Events branch, we all work together. The events department is in charge of planning everything, the confections department, which I have been in charge of since it opened, the jewelry department and finally, the beauty department, which is in charge of making beauty products that are more original than the ones we used to use and of pampering our clients.

Everything goes through the event department which is in charge of informing us of the next requests. Personally, this system suits me a lot. We don't have to all meet at the same time to meet the bride and groom and take their requests into account. We work together, each at our own pace without stressing ourselves.

Jayna joins me as we enter the company building.

"The meeting will start in 10 minutes in room 1. Almost everyone has arrived."

"Jay, what are you talking about ? Don't tell me it's the annual meeting already."

"Alma, you're wearing me out," my secretary sighed. "The president's here for the annual meeting as usual."

"Oh. I forgot to tell you. I'm not going."

"What do you mean you're not going? We talked about this before. I'm not asking you to go. I'm just letting you know you will go."

"Jay. Remember what happened last year ? I thought I was going to be fired after screwing up my presentation," I said as I continued to walk. "Let's not go."

"Keep walking and dreaming. We're going to this meeting."

We enter the meeting room already filled. The door opens and the president enters followed by his secretary. All the people in the room stand up in unison to greet the president. I do the same, frowning.

This man scares me for no reason. He just has that thing about him, the way he stands, the way he walks and his glare. I've never seen him smile at work.

The secretary whispers something to the president who nods before starting the meeting. The secretary leaves the room quietly. I wonder where he is going again.

It's my turn to speak. Everybody is looking at me. It's so stressful. I hate talking in public. Whatever. The faster I start, the faster I'll get to sit down.

"As you have seen, handmade wedding dresses with meticulous details are more and more trendy. That's why we decided to take new stylists on trial to gain efficiency. . ."

After half an hour of talking, I'm finally finished with my presentation.

"Thank you for your attention. Do you have any questions?"

The president quickly raises his hand before speaking.

"How long does it take to make one dress so that we have to hire new designers?"

"About a three months, if we work without overtime for simple embroideries. It depends on the number of people working on the dress and the complexity of the design. Recently, it took us three months with four people working on the details while working overtime to finish on time."

"Very good. Hire as many new people as necessary. That will be all, thank you."

A sigh of relief escapes me. The meeting finally ends. I look at my watch, it's already 12:00. I have about an hour and a half left to eat.

The doors of room open and the secretary comes back with Gabrielo. Our gazes meet and he smiles at me. What the fuck is he doing here ?

I hadn't seen him since Saturday, but he's as charismatic as ever.

"I'm sorry for being late."

He takes a seat at the end of the table with the president. My brain is trying to think of all the possible options.

"Everyone, I have the honor to introduce you to my son," the president says, smiling. "This is Gabrielo Moretti. He will be the CEO as from today. That's the end of this meeting."

I slept with the boss' son.

I even married him. I pack up my things so I can get out. I hear a throat clearing in the room.

Only Gabrielo and I are left.

"Mr. Moretti? Is there anything I can do to help you?"

"You can start by calling me by my first name. It's time to have lunch."

"I have a question before that. Did you know I worked at Dynasty?"

"I did," he says, coming closer. "Since this morning actually. I just got the list of people working in Dynasty. And your name was on it."

"Are you still okay about having lunch together ? And meeting my mom ?"

"What if I'm not ready ?"

"I'll call off. We can just go and have lunch by ourselves."

"But she's your mom." "And I married you. The least I can do is not putting you in an unconfortable situation. So yes, I will tell her to go home if you're not ready."

He takes his phone and start scrolliing. I put my hand on his and shake my head.

"Let's go."

We are in the car and Gabrielo is driving. I picked up my gift on the way to the parking lot and fixed my makeup. The disaster on my face following our little scene in the meeting room has been taken care of.

"Stop stressing," Gabrielo reassured me, taking my hand.

"Easy to say," I retorted, squeezing his hand. "You're not the one meeting your mother-in-law in ten minutes when you got married this Friday to someone you met in a nightclub. And whose feelings for you you don't even know."

"It's true that when you put it like that... I already told you that everything would be okay. I married you because I fell in love with you. All I have to do now is lure you into my arms."

I smile at him and he stops the car for a moment to kiss me.

"Now raise your head and smile," he said, raising my head with his index finger. "We're here and you're going to do great."

He kisses my hand before stopping the car.

Chapter 6

After entering the restaurant, we go directly to the first floor. The first thing I noticed was the lack of clients. Before noticing the flowering trees present in the room and the relaxing atmosphere that reigned there. It's almost magical. It feels like a fairy tale.

The room was completely empty except for one person with their back to us. We approached and I could finally see their face. A woman with ebony hair very similar to her son's, not to mention their crystal colored eyes.

Gabrielo's mother is breathtaking." Literally." I have rarely seen such a beautiful and elegant woman in my entire career as a fashion designer no matter how short it is." Even more so at her age." She glows and doesn't have a single wrinkle." She looks up in our direction and quickly approaches us."

"Mom, this is-"

"Quiet! I don't think I talked to you. Besides not inviting me to your wedding, I'm only meeting my daughter-in-law now."

I am... Speechless. This woman seems to have quite a temper. Not to mention the way Gabrielo avoids her gaze."

"Nice to meet you, my dear," she says, turning to me with a smile." Who would have thought that my son would finally get married? And with such a beautiful woman on top of that."

She takes me in her arms and draws me to sit next to her.

"Tell me, what do you want to eat?" She asks while taking the menu in her hands.

I watch her order along with Gabrielo and the waiters arrive in short notice. We start to eat with Gabrielo's mother who asks me questions from time to time.

"Now tell me...When will I have grandchildren?"

I choked up when I heard his question. Children? Although I've never asked myself that question, it's always seemed obvious to me that I'd have children one day. Even more so now that I'm married. Gabrielo hands me my glass of water and I thank him while drinking the water."

"Things will be done in time, Mom. Alma is still young, not to mention the fact that her career has just begun. Give her time."

"It's true," she admits. "Don't you want to have children yet? With my stupid son who refuses to face the truth, I risk dying before I can see his children."

Rosaria, my mother-in-law, has bright eyes and a pained look.

"Not at all! "I smile. "It's just that we've never talked about it. I, we're going to have kids eventually, don't worry."

"Do you really think so?"

"Absolutely!"

Rosaria hugs me and Gabrielo sighs as he watches his mother's behavior. I smile as I see their relationship. They get along much better than I ever got along with my family. I kind of envy them.

"Alma dear," Rosaria calls, "do not listen to my son. He didn't hear from me for over a month. His poor mother waited for him to come to visit her without him deigning to call me even once."

"Always in exaggeration," Gabrielo blows loud enough to be heard.

"I dare you to say that again," his mother threatens. "Even that stupid big brother of yours calls me once in a month!"

I couldn't help but laugh as I watched these two bickering like children. Rosaria smiles at me and continues to criticize her son. I accidentally hit my bag and suddenly remember my gift. I hand it to my mother-in-law nervously."

"You really didn't have to do that," she exclaimed, thanking me." I arranged this meeting overnight, not to mention that I have nothing for you. We're going shopping to make up for it!"

"I heard you liked jewelry. I hope you like it."

Rosaria opens the box before discovering the earring gem." She lets out a scream as she turns to me."

"Are these the real thing?" She asks as she alternates her gaze from the jewelry to my face.

"Of course they are. These are the Eternal Twins from Graff House." There has never been a piece of jewelry quite like it on this scale. A true masterpiece of craftsmanship in the field of jewelry.

She takes me in her arms and thanks me. I return her embrace smiling before loosening up. She turns to Gabrielo and rolls her eyes.

"I'll wear them to your wedding, she says, tucking them carefully into her purse. If my son deigns to lose a day in his life for an important event."

Gabrielo looks away and suddenly focuses on his phone screen. Ah. Is that how it is?

" No wedding, no house," I said, smiling at him. "What do you have to say? Say the right thing, or you'll be living as a bachelor all your life."

"Are you serious?" he asked, scrutinizing me.

" Do I look like I'm kidding? I didn't sign a paper to not celebrate anything at the end, believe me." Rosaria bursts out laughing when she sees her son's dejected look. He gives her a glare that she wipes away with a wave of her hand.

" Very well. The wedding will take placce in the near future," he gives in with a sigh.

"I believe that I am going to leave you now. Gabrielo," she says when hugging her son, "take care of my daughter-in-law. Do not call me before having good news to tell me."

In no time she leaves the restaurant, taking with her a dessert. What a woman! Gabrielo turns to me and changes his seat to sit next to me.

"A wedding?" He asks one last time.

" A huge ceremony actually. It is going to be time to go back to the office soon. Let's go," I say, standing up.

"Just a moment, ma'am," Gabo exclaims, grabbing me by the hips to sit on his lap. "We had to talk about a certain apartment to buy in the next few days."

"Really?" I said, feigning ignorance. "I thought we had to get married first."

"Well, stop believing now because we're going now."

"Where to?"

"On Maddison Avenue." A two-story penthouse. What do you think of that?"

"I trust you on that. For now, let me go, I need to go finish a dress at an emergency wedding."

"Not yet," he refuses, holding me tighter to him. "I can't believe it. I'm married and the only time I touched you was on the wedding night. What kind of fiasco is this?"

" Yours," I replied with a laugh." Now I really have to go before the bride has a nervous breakdown. I'll see you later!"

I quickly left the restaurant and called a cab to the ceremony venue. Two hours later, I return to my office to work. It drops me off quickly in front of Destiny's building. I go upstairs to start working on my latest sketch.

The door opens with a bang and I jump violently. Who is it that opens the door like that? Just as I was about to open the door, I met the gaze of the person in my office. What the hell is she doing here?

I thought we wouldn't see each other for at least a few more months.

"Is that how you greet your mother?"

Chapter 7

"What do you mean 'greet you'?" I asked as I looked at my puzzled mother. "What are you doing here?"

"I came to see my daughter who has been ignoring me for three days," she said, sitting down at my desk.

"You should have saved yourself the trouble. You clearly know why I didn't answer."

"Your sister is getting married to James in four months."

"And? You talk as if it's any of my business."

"Of course it is, because you're coming. Your presence is required. Try to find a partner till then."

"Let me just say this. I. Will. Not. Attend. Anything."

My mother rises to face me from the top of her heels.

"Trust me, you'll come. Your grandmother is getting sicker day by day. She said she won't get her heart surgery done before she sees you."

My grandmother. The only person in this family who genuinely cares about me. I can't afford to lose her just because I don't want to come. And my mother knows that.

"When is the surgery supposed to be performed?"

"Just after Mila and James wedding. It can't be sooner for some reason."

"Then we'll see," I replied, walking around the desk. "I won't be attending this wedding. Now, get the fuck out of my sight."

I call security to get my mother out of my office once and for all. I'll have to go to Spain in four months, maybe even before. I'd better get back to work for now.

After a while and several snack breaks, Gabrielo came knocking on my door. He walked in quietly before wrapping his arms around me.

"Mrs Moretti, it's time to go home. Your husband is waiting for you, not to mention the fact that he's hungry and it's getting late."

"All right, just let me finish this part of the dress before you go."

Gabrielo sits on one of the chairs in the room while he waits for me to finish. I continue to embroider and inlay the diamond fragments on the upper part of the dress. I only have a few things left to do before the fittings tomorrow. That's it! Perfect.

" We can go now," I announced as I opened the door to my office.

Gabrielo leads us to his car, which is parked in the hallway. The driver opens the door for us to sit down. I thank him and sit down properly.

" I heard that you sent someone out through security," Gabrielo begins. "Did something bad happen ?"

" It was my mother. She had come to tell me that I was needed at my sister's wedding. Unfortunately," I sighed.

Gabrielo gives me a puzzled look.

"My 'sister' is marrying my ex. Ex who cheated on me with her for over a year," I added with a bitter smile. "I don't think my presence at her wedding is necessary."

Gabrielo's expression is mixed. I can see anger, sorrow and perhaps a little sympathy. I can't figure out what he's thinking. As strange as it sounds. I mean, it's not like I can read people's minds.

" You're going?" he asks, taking my hand and bringing it to his lips.

"Correction: I'm planning to visit my sick grandmother," I sighed, feeling a migraine coming on. "She didn't really leave me much choice after involving my grandmother in this story."

"I'm coming with you," Gabrielo concluded.

"I wasn't planning on leaving without you," I said with a grin.

"I hope so. When are we leaving?

"In about four months.

"Stop pouting," he said, entering a building. "Besides, you've never told me why you're so keen for us to move into a new flat."

" It's just that I think that to start a new life, having a new house is essential. Even more so because we're married. I want to do things right."

" What a dreamer! Who knew I married a dreamer wedding dress designer," he laughs. "Did all those weddings made you all dreamy?"

" That's not true," I said, tapping him on the shoulder. "Where are we anyway?"

" In our new house," he announces, winking at me.

" Don't tell me that..."

" Yes, I bought the flat earlier. Now all we have to do is move in. What do you think?"

" It's amazing," I said looking around us." And my things? They're all still at home."

"I brought it all back here," he announced, opening my car door. "If you don't mind, ma'am."

He holds out his hand and I grab it without hesitation. We walk down the hall and all eyes are on us. It's true that we have to be a bit flashy with Gabo, who is almost 6'4 tall and has an imposing stature.

We enter the lift that gives access to the flat. This place is simply incredible. A mixture of modern and ancient. Not to mention the fact that the famous penthouse spans two floors. I jump into his arms and thank him again.

" Now," Gabrielo begins, lifting me up, "it's time to enjoy my second wedding night."

" Is it? I still have work to do. And we agreed to wait a little longer.

" Is everything alright? If something bothers you, you can just tell me and we'll try to fix it together. You know ?"

" I know that. I just need time to adjust to this whole new situation."

" All right. Wait a second," he asks as he walks away. "I have something to show you."

He walks up the stairs and stops in front of a marble door. After pushing the door open, I discover the master bedroom. This room is huge. I can't believe it, it's as big as my bedroom and dressing room.

" The master bedroom. Our room," Gabrielo insists. "If it's okay with you."

I nod and take a look around. I feel like I'm dreaming.

" All your stuff has been moved here. Do you like it?"

" Very much," I say, smiling earnestly.

" Get changed for now," Gabrielo says, laying me on the bed. "I'm going to make some food."

He leaves the room after removing his coat and tie. I watch him leave and close the door behind to start changing. My phone rings and I stop to answer Meavy.

" Hello?"

" In three words, your meeting with your mother-in-law."

" Surprise. Pleasant and... Original."

" What did you get her?" Meavy asks curiously.

It's true I didn't tell her what I was going to get Rosaria.

" The pair of Eternal Twins."

" Excuse you," Meavy shouts across the line, making me wince. "What did she get ?"

" The immaculate, identical 50 carat stones where you can see yourself as if in a mirror", I describe.

" You gave it to her! What about me? You don't love me anymore? I knew it!"

"She's my mother-in-law. As long as I can't afford the millions of dollars to get a divorce, I'm gonna be good to her," I replied, smiling.

If only I could see her face to laugh. She can be such a drama queen when she wants.

" Alma!"

" What?"

" You know very well how much I wanted these earrings," Meav' whined. "They're one of a kind."

" Too bad, you're not my mother-in-law. Stop whining. Meav', I'll get you something nice for your birthday. Okay?"

" Okay. But you better impress me."

" Don't worry about it I'll..."

Boom! I hear a scream coming from downstairs.

" Meav', I'll leave you. I've let my husband go 'cook' and I think he made a mess downstairs."

" Go ahead. I'll call you tomorrow. I'll see you Friday for our coffee?"

" Perfect. Love you." I hurry to put on my slippers and get down the stairs. With a bit of luck, Gabrielo should still be in one piece.

I hope so.

Chapter 8

[Alma's dress above]

" You should have told me if you didn't know how to cook."

" Ouch!" Gabrielo cries with a grimace. "A little softer, you'll cut off my blood flow."

" If you didn't want to suffer, you shouldn't have cut the palm of your hand. Now let me do it."

Gabrielo continues to flinch with each spray of antiseptic. Even though it was a good idea, he should have told me that he couldn't cook. Or how to use a knife at all.

" That's it," I said, getting up. "I'm going to finish, or rather, start making dinner."

" Okay, I'll go and shower. Thanks, Alma."

Gabrielo places a kiss on my forehead and turns back to our room. I feel a smile crack my face. I think this marriage is going to work out.

Finally, the weekend! I've been waiting for this day all week. It's time to go see Meavy! I have been waiting for this moment all day. Even more so because today we are doing our Sweets Time at my house. And she still doesn't know I moved out.

Gabrielo is working overtime to get on with some urgent projects. I bought our weekly snack and drinks. Not to mention this week's gossip. Everything is ready, I just have to wait for Meav' to come and get me.

" Hi babe!" Meavy exclaims, jumping on me.

" Hey, shall we go?"

" Absolutely!"

Meavy starts her car and I type the address into the GPS.

" You moved out without telling me?" Meavy is astonished, giving me her famous outraged look.

" More than just moving, I moved in with my husband."

Meavy slams on the brake, making me jump from my seat.

" Meavy!"

" What? You've moved in with your husband. We need to celebrate!"

" No nightclubs," I replied. "I've had enough for the rest of the year, maybe even my life."

" Killjoy. For once, you could forget your problems," Meavy growled.

" The last time you advised me to go to a club to forget my problems, I ended up married. Forever."

" Alma," Meavy cries. "I'm begging you as a friend! Be a good person and come with me for one last night of debauchery."

Debauch my eye. The only thing you care about is finding something to do for the evening. I'd rather stay home, away from the trouble you're going to cause me.

We get out of the car and take the lift up to the flat. We sit in front of the flat screen in the living room, glued together, sharing a huge tub of ice cream. After a long time, I hear footsteps coming towards us.

The movie we are watching becomes quiet while the two protagonists get closer and the psychopath follows them without them noticing. He raises his arm and is about to stab them. The girl turns around and he jumps on her. A clearing of the throat makes us both jump on the spot. We jump into each other's arms with tears in our eyes.

" Is my wife being stolen from me now?" Gabrielo asks, coming to kiss my cheek when he returns as usual.

"She's better off with me, just like in the film," Meavy replies. Look at that.

The girl's girlfriend knocks out the psychopath with a bottle of wine and ends up stabbing him with it. She picks up her wounded girlfriend in the stomach and kisses her.

"Is this the particular reason you're watching lesbian romance?"

I turn to Gabrielo before slapping his shoulder.

"Anyway, I French-kissed Alma first, so calm down."

Gabo gives me a weird look before starting to head for the exit.

" Meavy!" I yelled as I threw myself at her. "This was supposed to stay between us!"

" But! It's the truth. By the way," she began, turning to my husband, "are you coming to the club with us?"

" I've got work to do tomorrow," he says apologetically.

" See, I told you he was busy," I insisted.

" But I can do it later if you really want to go," Gabrielo adds with a shrug.

" Yeah! To the club!"

Meavy runs through our living room without stopping. Hopefully she'll stop before she throws up her ice cream. I take the jar back into my hands to finish it. Might as well minimize the waste. My best friend goes up to our room and I am left alone with Gabrielo.

" Why?" I asked, grabbing Gabo's arm. "The last time I was in a club, I got married. Married !"

I shake him by the shoulders as he sits on the sofa smiling. I fall next to him and he wraps his arms around me before bringing his face close to mine. My heart leaps into my rib cage and I feel my breathing quicken.

" What's wrong? Embarrassed?" he asks, raising an eyebrow.

" Not at all," I say, bringing my face closer to kiss him.

" ALMA! COME HERE!" Meavy shouts from upstairs.

I stop in my tracks and break away from Gabo's embrace. Meavy is waiting for me in our room with four different outfits.

" Which one? Quickly, I have to finish getting ready and get you ready. The perfect man could appear out of nowhere."

" For you. Let me remind you, I am married. So if you want to find your soul mate, it'll be without me."

" Pfft, always here to crush the mood and my dreams. Poor me."

" Yeah, yeah, yeah. Get dressed faster because after 11:00, I'm not stepping foot outside."

" All right, just wait a moment."

We both walk down the stairs towards the living room. Gabrielo is on the phone and seems rather relaxed. He sees us coming and hangs up without delay.

" Are you ready?"

" Always, we answer in unison."

" Alma, where are you headed in this dress?" Gabrielo asks with a tense smile.

" In a nightclub," I answered quickly. "My husband decided we should go without consulting me, so I'm going. People can admire your wife. Be happy."

He becomes silent and approaches me. Meav' has gone out to get her car when we wait here. Gabrielo kisses me on the forehead and hugs me.

"I'm sorry, okay? I thought you'd want to go out tonight. Even more so now that your friend is here. Now, don't you want to cover up a bit more? You're going to catch a cold."

" It's Meavy and I don't really feel like going to a club tonight. Anyway, you've already said yes to her, so forget it. Let's go before we make her wait too long."

" Let's go," he mumbles, holding onto my waist.

" Alma," Gabrielo calls out in my ear. "How about we go sit down?"

" You should relax," I say, looking at his tense face.

" With what?"

A mischievous smile appears on Gabo's face.

" With a cocktail you'll like. Come on!"

We sit down at the bar and I order our drinks. A "Lady's Leg Cosmopolitan" for me and "The Versailles Experience" for Gabrielo. He should like it, I think.

" How's that?"

" Not bad."

" I knew it. Shall we dance?"

" Let's go," he says, holding out his hand.

Gabrielo leads me onto the dance floor and new music starts. Time passes and our dance turns into a game of seduction. I feel my body moving against his in a harmonious way and I can't do anything about it. Our faces get closer to each other before our lips meet...

Chapter 9

We pull away from each other and look at each other. I think it's the first time in my life someone has given me a look like that. Filled with tenderness, affection and desire.

"What's the matter? Gabrielo asks, resting his forehead against mine. "You're frowning."

" Nothing important. It's just that... I'll tell you about it when I get home. How about we just keep dancing?"

" "I'll be fine, thanks. For now," he says, lifting me in his arms, "we're going home."

I get carried to the car where the driver is already waiting for. The car starts and an awkward silence reigns in the cabin. I feel Gabrielo's burning gaze on my skin, but I don't dare turn my head to look at him. We arrive in front of the building and Gabrielo gets out and opens the door for me.

He carries me back in and heads for the lift. All eyes in the hall turn to us. I hear some whispers that make me hide my flushed face in Gabrielo's neck. The lift opens and we arrive in the flat.

"Can you tell me what's wrong now?" Gabrielo asks as he puts me down on the sofa.

"Is that why we left like that? And Meavy? I didn't even say goodbye."

"Stop thinking about Meavy," Gabrielo retorts. "She saw us leave and she waved at me while she was dancing. Come to the point."

" I was afraid."

" Of what?"

" Of sleeping with you," I admitted with my head down. "I couldn't shake the idea that maybe if we were sober you'd change your mind. Or that you'd leave afterwards, or then-"

Gabrielo cuts me off with a hug. He kisses my head. I close my eyes and he holds my face with both hands as if I'm going to fly away. He reaches my lips and moves them in unison against mine. They are so soft, soon I feel his tongue against my lips. I open my mouth to catch my breath and he takes the opportunity to slip his tongue in.

He changes my position and lays me on the huge sofa. His hands go down behind my back, grabbing my thigh to pull me closer to him. I feel his body against mine, unable to part from him.

Air.

I need air.

Gabrielo seems to get the message and pulls away from me. I catch my breath, totally out of breath. Meanwhile, he moves towards my neck where he places kisses without pausing. I feel him tugging at my skin discreetly.

" Let me tell you something," he said, lifting his head to look me in the eye. "You're the only person I've ever been attracted to in my entire life. No matter how hard I tried, I couldn't get you out of my head."

"What do you mean by 'your entire life'?"

"I looked for you for so long I thought it was all over," he laughs. "I'm glad I met you again. You don't know how much I wanted to meet you again." I hug him at the loss of words.

"What do you like so much about me?"

"I love your dark eyes," he says, placing a kiss on every part of my body he mentions. "Your face, your belly, your stretch marks that tend to make you complex. Not to mention your repartee, your lovely smile and the way you make me feel at ease around you. I love you as you are. So let me show you."

I try catching my breath when Gabrielo lifts me and goes straight to our bedroom.

My alarm clock chimes on the bedside table and I put my hand down to stop it. I just need five more minutes, for God's sake. I feel like there is a weight in my brain. I look for Gabrielo on the bed, but my hand meets only the cold sheets instead.

Where has he gone? I open my eyes, still foggy from sleep, and start looking around the room. The bathroom door opens revealiing Gabrielo dripping with water, a towel around his waist. I can see a drop of water running down his chest and getting lower and lower.

" Enjoying the view?"

" Very much. I married you, enjoying the view is the least I can do," I say as I stand up to reach him.

Ow! This was a bad idea. I'm still sore from the night before and my legs are giving out on me. I grimace as I bend in half. Gabrielo grabs me as and helps me sit up again.

" Easy, there. I think you'd better rest for today."

" No, no, no, no. I'll be fine. I'll go to work. I've got some important appointments scheduled."

" Alma," he sighs, "the most important thing is you, so rest. You obviously need to rest today."

" I'll rest at noon. I will. I really have to go. I've got to go to some ceremonies to see if there's anything wrong with the wedding gowns. I'd hate it if there was a problem because I didn't show up."

" All right, fine. We'll have lunch together. You'll take your two-hour break like everyone else. For now, let's run a warm bath. That'll help."

I nod quickly before being carried to the bath. Half an hour later I'm ready to go to work. Gabrielo takes me to the office with him so I can rest. I kiss him as I get out of the car before hurrying to meet Jayna. Everything is going to be fine even if he doesn't believe me.

The meetings with the bride and groom went smoothly this morning. All I have to do now is finish the afternoon's meetings and everything will be over. It's lunchtime and my secretary Jayna asks me to join the others but I have to decline her offer.

" I have already promised to have lunch with someone else. I'll come next time and invite you, okay?"

" No problem, don't forget your promise. See you later," she exclaims, waving at me.

Now I have to go and see Gabrielo. I head for the lift in the middle of the corridor before going to the top floor. I'm doing much better than this morning. I think the warm bath really helped. The secretary on the floor stares at me before calling out to me.

" Miss? Can I have your name and check if you have an appointment."

"Sure. I'm Alma Pearson," I answered, pulling out my phone.

I text Gabrielo to tell him I've arrived. He leaves on seen without answering. Great.

A man in a suit gets out of the lift and asks me to follow him. We walk through countless corridors before arriving in a huge office.

"I've got this, Sheila," he says to the secretary. "The president is in a meeting at the moment, he will arrive any moment. He asks you to wait in here."

The man leaves the room and a few minutes later my dear husband enters the room. He walks over to me and kisses me as usual.

"Where do you want to eat ?"

" To the Melt Shop!"

We quickly arrive at the fast-food and our orders arrive. I eat quietly when Gabrielo catches my attention.

" Don't tell me you've never eaten in a fast-food before ?"

" No, I've eaten there before. It's just that it's been so long since I've eaten in here. It's weird."

I grab a fry from his tray and point it at his mouth.

" Say 'Ahhh'."

Gabrielo is reluctant but finally opens his mouth and starts eating.

" Alma?"

" Yes?"

" Let's go on a honeymoon."

Hello everyone! This is the first time I'm talking to you here.

I would like to ask you, where do you think Alma and Gabo will go on their honeymoon?

I want to hear your most original ideas !Kisses!

Chapter 10

"A honeymoon," I asked, completely speechless. "Where to?"

"We can think about that later," Gabrielo replied smiling. "For now, I just want to know if you're interested in the idea."

"I like it, that's for sure."

"Then it's decided," Gabrielo concludes beaming. "We're leaving in a fortnight. How about the Caribbean?"

"Let's get it out in the open, I wouldn't set foot on an island. No matter what it is. Have you never seen movies about shipwrecks ? How about Italy?"

"I'm not going to visit a country I grew up in", he complains. "If I go, I might as well discover something."

"Why don't we talk about it later?" I suggested. "I'd like to take advantage of the little free time you have."

What I just said sounded more like a reproach than anything else. Gabrielo looks down at his plate.

"Gabo, I-"

"I know, you didn't want it to come out this way. It doesn't matter."

"Of course it does. I am sorry. It's just that right now, you're so busy that I'd like to take time to enjoy being with you. And get to know you a little better."

"Let's do something. As soon as the European contract is signed, I'll have a lot more free time. For now, think of a destination for our honeymoon, huh? I'll stay with you for as long as you want."

Gabrielo grabs my hand and places a kiss on it. I feel my cheeks silently blush. He smiles mischievously and releases my hand. We finish eating in good spirits.

"Shall we go back to the office?"

I nod, still on a cloud as Gabo leads me to the car. The ride passes in a comfortable silence while I admire the landscape.

"We've arrived," Gabrielo announces, bringing me out of my thoughts.

"Thanks for the ride! See you tonight," I greeted, kissing him on the lips.

I slam the car door behind me and rush to my office. My meeting starts in less than ten minutes and I'm not ready. Jayna beckons me from her office to come in.

"Relax, we're on time. The meeting will be delayed by fifteen minutes at the request of the planning department. The bookings have been non-stop since yesterday."

"Thank you, Jayna. Tell them I won't be taking any applications that need to be done after the next two weeks. I will only take the important ones. I'm going on holiday in a fortnight."

"That's pretty rare," she says. "Don't tell me you've found someone?"

"Yes, I have! You'll meet him soon enough. Meavy has already met him."

"Seriously? Can't wait to know the person that chose to handle you while sober. Now that I think about it, when are you planning to leave for your sister's wedding?"

"As late as possible," I mumbled. "I'm already going, I wouldn't want to come early. That'll be the last straw in this whole thing."

"Your relationship is still as explosive as ever, I guess. I'll leave you to it. All the documents for the meeting are on your desk."

I thank Jayna before I get back to work.

Where the hell am I gonna go on this honeymoon?

After several discussions and debates on the subject, we have agreed on a destination. During our three-week stay, we are going to make the most of our time together. I will finally be able to spend time alone with my man!

My bags are already packed as we leave in two hours. I want this trip to be memorable and above all, far from work. That's why I've hidden my computer and Gabrielo's in the house. Let's hope he doesn't find out until we're gone.

"Alma," Gabrielo calls out from upstairs, "where are my suits?"

Ah. . I was expecting this question. Well, it's time to tell him what happened to his clothes. I go upstairs to our room before heading to the dressing room. Gabrielo is standing in the middle of the room.

"Hey," I say, giving him a hug from behind.

"What's wrong with you?" Gabrielo asks without turning around.

"Me? Nothing. It's just that I thought you'd be better off without a suit for the trip. It's too flashy, not to mention that we're supposed to be relaxing."

"Alma, where are my clothes?"

"At Meavy's? I replied with a smile."

"Sweetheart, why would my clothes be at her place?" he asked a little too quietly.

"Don't worry," I answered hastily to divert his attention. "They're safe there. She'll put them back here when we get back."

It's better for both of us to stay in the dark. I know Meavy needed them, but as to why, I have no idea. I don't even want to know.

"Anyway," I said, "we're leaving and you'd better get dressed. I've put some clothes for you in the bathroom, come on!"

We are currently on the plane. Gabrielo has fallen asleep with my head already on his shoulder. He must be exhausted and so am I.

I've spent the worst two weeks of my life making and fitting dresses last minute. Not to mention rearranging and moving appointments. Jayna looked like she was having a nervous breakdown lately. We worked non-stop until the last second and were working overtime.

Now that I'm on holiday, so is she. Fortunately for both of us, the next three weeks will give us a chance to rest. I thought I was going to die.

When I think about it, I've been married to Gabrielo for two months already. A lot has happened since then. I've even got used to living with him. We have our own routine and it's fine with me. Which is suprising because I hate routine.

"Alma?" Gabrielo calls.

"Yeah?"

" Can you remind me why we didn't take a private jet when we have a 15-hour flight?" he asks, already irritated.

"Because you need to get out of your comfort zone once in a while. Look at you. You're wearing clothes that look your age and you're on a plane in business class. That's a good start."

"I could have done without it, honestly. And slept in a bed. With you," he says, whining in my ear.

"If it makes you feel better," I say, sitting on top of him and leaning into his ear, "I'll make it up to you while we're there. Gabrielo, do you want to have children? I mean later. Not now."

"I'd love to. My mother is still waiting for our children and so am I. I'd rather enjoy making them for the time being. What about you?"

"I really like children. They are all just lovely and surprising. I definitely wanna be a mom one day."

"We can get started right now." Gabo suggests.

"To make what?"

"Children."

"Not here, that's for sure," I replied laughing.

He starts laughing too. He puts his hands behind my back. I rest my head on his chest to enjoy the moment. Sometimes silence is better than talking.

"What do you think of our destination," I ask to change the subject.

"I haven't been there yet, but it sounds like a good idea."

There is a comfortable silence and I start playing on my phone.

"Where's my computer?"

"In your suitcase," I answer without thinking. Oh. "We agreed not to do any work so I left it at home."

"Alma..."

"No. You need to rest and clear your head for now. And that's what we'll do. I'll even help you do it."

Fortunately for us, each pair of seats is privatized by tinted, soundproof glass walls. Gabrielo refuses to meet my gaze. I place a kiss on his cheek before moving lower. Neck, Adam's apple, collarbone. I unbutton his shirt and continue down his torso. He grabs my chin just as I reach his trousers.

"Fine," he sighs, lifting my head before kissing me. "You'd better stop if you don't want to start something here."

I smile and return to my seat as if nothing had happened. Gabrielo buttons up his shirt and takes a deep breath before giving me a lustful look. Too bad for him, we're on a plane. A stewardess enters and serves us lunch.

We start to eat and it seems that I still don't like the mussels. Their texture disgusts me more than anything else. I attack my dessert before turning to Gabrielo.

"Gabo, would you give me your dessert?"

"What do I get in return?" he asks, raising an eyebrow.

"Anything you want."

"Then I want you. For a whoel night."

He smiles and hands me his plate without adding anything. At the same time he asks one of the hostesses to bring more dessert. I jump on him and give him a hug.

"Thank you, I love you! I knew you wouldn't let me starve."

"I love you too, now start eating," he replies, stroking my hair.

The desserts arrive in less than a minute and I start eating. Nothing like sugar to make you feel good. Even more so with the long drive ahead of us.

"Attention please, the flight to New Delhi, India is about to land. All passengers are requested to return to their seats and fasten their seat belts."

Chapter 11

The plane lands safely on the ground and we land in India. I finally stretch before going to collect my luggage with Gabrielo.

"Where do we sleep?" I ask as Gabrielo takes my suitcase from my hand.

"In the middle of Old Delhi for three days then we are going to Udaipur. It's a place filled in Indian culture. At least, that's what google said. We'll stay in a suite at Haveli Dharampura."

"Let's take a taxi then."

"I took care of the car. Let's go."

A car is waiting for us outside the airport. Gabrielo takes out the keys and opens it without lingering. We get in and head for Haveli Dharampura. The jet lag of 9 hours disturbs me a lot. It's already getting dark here while it's not even 7 am in New York.

I am still tired from the trip. Although I slept the whole way. I feel exhausted. The journey goes on quietly with the sound of the radio in the background. When the car stops, I get out without lingering.

We finally arrive in the suite and I fall back against the bed. I feel like I deserve to rest. Gabo joins me on the bed and positions himself behind me before taking me in his arms. He starts playing with the button on my jeans and finally undoes it.

"Can I ?" he whispers in my ear, making me shiver.

"I just want to sleep for today. Tomorrow ? "

"Sure, sweet dreams," he says, placing a kiss on my forehead as my eyes close.

The sun streams in through the windows and beats down on my face. I look at the time on my phone and sit down on the bed. Nausea hits me and I take a deep breath. The few hours of sleep I managed to get weren't enough apparently. I feel like I've been to Fashion Week and it just ended.

I'm going to feel sick all day. It's always the same whenever my sleep cycle is disrupted. I'd better go back to sleep, it's not even 5 o'clock yet. I'll be fine when I wake up.

Conclusion: I did not wake up feeling worse. I feel better, but nothing more.

Gabrielo is still sleeping soundly. He is lovely when he sleeps like that. He should rest more often. I run my hand through his hair. It's really silky. Maybe even more than mine.

"Alma," Gabrielo grumbles. "Stop it, let me sleep."

"It's already ten o'clock. Wake up so we can go and eat. I'm hungry."

"You're not. You're still sleepy that's why you're so confused. Come here."

He pulls me to him and puts his head on my chest. I think he's fallen asleep again. Come on, just a few minutes won't hurt us.

That's what I thought until we woke up at 12. I'm starving. All because of Gabrielo.

"Shall we go?" Gabo asks, taking me by the hand.

I get up and we go out for lunch. The streets are already crowded with people and the surrounding noise is deafening. We go to Paranthe Wali Gali to taste some culinary specialities. It is a narrow and famous street of Chandni Chowk crowded with people coming to eat in the restaurants.

The smell of oil and food fills the atmosphere all around us. My stomach starts rumbling and luckily for me, the noise around us covers the one of my stomach. The din of shopkeepers calling for customers fills the air as people scramble to fill their plates with more and more food.

It is said that the recipes offered by some of the stalls are generations old. I can't wait to try it. We sit inside a stall and order Indian paranthas and rolls.

It's simply delicious. Even for me, who is not a fan of food, the Indian food might change my mind. Gabrielo seems to enjoy it from the smile on his face. We finish eating and leave the shop. The sun is beating down on the street and it's getting hot.

"Gabrielo, what about dessert?"

"Do you still want to eat after that?" he asks in surprise.

"What do you mean 'after that'?" I said outraged. "Dessert is the most important course. Not to mention the fact that I ate less so I could eat dessert. So, please."

He sighs before putting his arm around my waist. He buys a red velvet cake and we eat it. If this trip goes on like this, I have a feeling I won't be going back anytime soon.

The rest of the afternoon was spent in food tasting and talking to locals. Afterwards, we decided to go to a sound and light show with a dinner show at the Red Fort in Delhi.

The Red Fort in Delhi is an icon of the city, with a history dating back over 300 years. The sound, light and dinner show is a unique blend of the old and the new. The show is choreographed by professionals. The show is professionally choreographed and features many historical events that are part of the region's heritage.

The evening also includes a locally prepared Indian meal. We were able to enjoy the show thanks to the incredible Indian dancers. The show was dazzling and captivating. Just thinking about it makes me want to dance.

We decided to go for a little digestive walk, because our place of residence is not far away.

"What are we doing tomorrow? Gabrielo asks.

"No idea," I answer. "We'll see at the time. It's late, we'll think about it when we wake up."

"Speaking of waking up, Mrs Moretti, we left something off last night."

"I know we did. Don't worry about it."

We reach the haveli by then. I hurry to the suite and lock myself in the bathroom. At least, that's what I thought I was doing. Until Gabrielo catches me in the middle of my run, carrying me like a sack of potatoes the whole way.

"Give me a moment, I'll be right back," I said, rushing into the bathroom. "I want to go to the bathroom."

If you're going to do things, you might as well do them right. That's why I've got a brand new set of lingerie to please Gabrielo and me too, by the way. I put on my new outfit and look at myself in the mirror. I like it. I look good in it. I hope he likes it. I spent a fortune to make him happy.

I breathe in and take a last look at myself in the mirror. I leave the room to face my husband. It seems he didn't hear me come out. He is still lying like a starfish on the bed. I climb on top of him and kiss him without wasting any time.

He turns me over under him and looks me up and down. I see his pupils dilate and he suddenly grabs my thighs to pull me closer. I give in to him and raise myself up slightly to kiss him. I have to say, I have been waiting for this.

Chapter 12

6 am. I am woken up by the noise of horns. I have barely had two hours of sleep. Drivers stuck at junctions keep honking their horns as they try to squeeze in somewhere. The traffic is clogged with rickshaws overloaded with goods and cars.

I watch passers-by zigzag between the cars trying not to get run over. Rickshaws race against dusty bicycles and cars on a broken road. Monkeys and cows are also making their way along the road. Everything is different here.

I sit down on the bed -well, I try- before lying down again. My thighs and stomach are so sore that just sitting down is painful. I think I'll stay on the bed for now. I thought I was used to spending the night with Gabrielo, but it seems that I am not.

Noises coming from the bathroom catch my attention. It's clear that Gabo is not on the bed. He comes out of the bathroom with a towel around his waist.

"Already awake?" he says surprised. "I thought you wanted to sleep."

"Correction. I do need to sleep. It's just too noisy for that to be possible, that's all."

"Poor thing," he exclaims as he approaches. "Do you want to carry on with what we did last night? I have plenty of time if it's for you."

"I'll be good. I'm so sore that even sitting down is painful."

"When I said you should start exercising again," he replied.

"Leave me alone. I'm in great shape. I don't need to go and sweat my ass off to make sure of that."

He plants a kiss on my forehead before carrying me in his arms.

"Gabrielo, no. Put me down. I'm really sore all over."

He puts me down slowly and I stand up as best I can. I move forward to take a step before bending over. Gabrielo puts me back to bed instantly. I try to keep a cool face but I can feel myself frowning.

"It looks like we'll be here all day."

"No, why?" I asked in disappointment.

"You're in pain. I can see it in your face. Besides, you're not going to get very far like this. Just rest. We've got three more weeks here."

I nod my head miserably. It's not like I'm going to convince him. I don't even have the strength to argue. I might as well sleep and rest for now. Besides, since he mentioned it, I really don't feel well. I've been feeling a migraine coming on since a while ago and the fatigue isn't helping.

Gabrielo gets back into bed with me and takes me in his arms. I rest my head against his chest and listen to his breathing. Somehow I already feel better. I'm sure that after a good nap I can go out and try some new Indian food.

Well, it looks like one nap wasn't enough. One day. That's how long it took me to recover. An entire day spent in the haveli without being able to go out, or move around as I pleased because Mister thought I should rest even after taking a warm bath.

Today we are going to walk around the streets of Mumbai and the bazaars of the city. We went to Udaipur for a few days and it was amazing. Since I am feeling better, I might as well enjoy it. Nothing like fresh air and good food to celebrate.

"Gabo, hurry up. Come on!"

"I'm coming," he say, quickening his pace. "You should slow down and avoid running like that. You'll end up with heatstroke."

"You always worry too much! I'll be fine."

Chor bazaar is one of the largest flea markets in India. The alleys are packed with stalls full of various goods. As legend has it, if any of your belongings have been stolen in Mumbai, then you will likely find it on sale at Chor Bazaar. I lead the way through the bazaar and Gabrielo follows me without question. We walk hand in hand without stopping.

"Alma, where are we going? We've been walking for a while."

"Have we? Do you think so," I asked, avoiding his gaze.

"Do you have any idea where we are?"

"Not at all, but as they say, 'it's by getting lost that one truly discovers the country'.

"Nobody says that, Stellina."

"Well, I do. I'll prove to you how true that is."

That's how I made my first friend in India. She showed us the way and made friends with us. So Mayra stayed with us all afternoon and we even had lunch at Cafe Madras.

This place has been running for over 80 years in Matunga. We tried their dosas, Idli and also their Sheera to end the meal on a sweet note.

"You should go out during Holi," Mayra exclaims.

"Holi?" I asked. "What is Holi?"

"It is a Hindu religious festival, which marks the end of winter and the beginning of spring. During Holi, everyone throws coloured powders and water on each other."

As I understand it, Holi has its origin in Hindu mythology. Legend has it that King Hiranyakashipu ruled as a despot, stirring up trouble around him. Proud and arrogant, he demanded that everyone prostrate themselves at his feet. Unfortunately for him, his own son Prahlad preferred the god Vishnu.

Hiranyakashipu wanted to get rid of his son. He tried several times to kill him, but in vain. He then asked for help from his sister Holika, who had the unique gift of not being afraid of fire. The king challenged his son to lie down in the flames with his aunt.

Prahlad accepted and triumphed. Holika was punished for her vanity while Prahlad was saved and rewarded by the gods for his faithfulness and devotion. From this story, Holi is said to have originated as a symbol of the victory of good over evil, fertility and the arrival of spring.

"On the eve of the festival, huge bonfires are lit throughout the city. They celebrate the cremation of Holika, sister of King Hiranyakashipu, and symbolise the destruction of evil. The coals are then collected by the inhabitants who take them home and use them to light a new fire."

"Sounds amazing! I can't wait to get there."

"Be careful what you wear. The mixture of powder and water makes a kind of indelible mud. It's hard to remove your clothes after Holi, believe me! " Mayra laughs.

"Don't worry! We'll be dressed properly, won't we Gabo?" He nods and smiles.

"I'm not worried. It's just that the main targets are women and tourists. The party is in a fortnight."

"It'll be just before we leave," I said.

"The day before we leave, so we should take advantage of it," Gabo replied.

"I'll see you lovebirds later ! Alma has my number. Sleep well and don't make too many children!"

I feel my face turn bright red. Gabrielo laughs at my reaction and takes my hand.

"Let's go home, it's getting late."

Chapter 13

Today is Holi.

And who says Holi, says colours!

Mayra called us the day before to suggest that we go back to Vrindavan with her to enjoy the festival. She was planning to go home for the festivities and we agreed to accompany her. That' s how we found ourselves out of our haveli and into another town.

We came all the way from New Delhi to here in Vrindavan to enjoy the festivities. This town has a special symbolism for a traditional holi after all. We will be staying at Mayra's family home for four days and three nights.

Today is Holi and tomorrow is our departure. Mayra's family has been very welcoming and warm. It felt like home. Mayra's mother advised me to put on some white kurta pyjamas for the Indian tradition and to highlight the colours.

- Don't forget that every colour has a meaning. Green represents harmony, orange represents optimism, blue represents vitality and red represents joy and love. Today, social barriers are falling, men and women are equal. Enjoy it, girls," says Mayra's mother.

- You will be able to taste dishes specially prepared for Holi," adds Mayra. There will even be thandai.

- What is thandai?

- A mixture of milk, almonds, spices and marijuana!

I slip a waterproof bag with my phone inside around my neck. At least it will stay in one piece. Gabrielo enters the room and hugs me. I feel like he's become more and more physical since we got here, not that I'm complaining. I feel like I need to touch him too actually.

- You might hear "Bura Na Mano, Holi Hai!" from everywhere. That's to say 'Don't be angry, it's Holi' when they throw powder at you," explains Mayra.

- Shall we go?

- Let's go. Mama! We're going out, see you later.

- Take care of yourself! Have fun!

We go out into the street and the sound of the intense music echoes off the walls. It is almost unbearable. The streets are full of people and only a few places are quiet. Children are splashing coloured water on each other with water pistols or filled balloons.

And of course the four of us were showered with a large bucket filled to the brim. Mayra's brother, runs after some of the children and sprays them with coloured powders. He comes back to us completely soaked and coloured.

A procession takes place to the temple, people gather around on foot, but also on motorbikes. A parade of men of different ages on the same motorbike passes us. They make a concert of horns while shouting intelligible words.

Troops of musicians make noise on their drums. Everyone is euphoric, greeting each other by applying coloured powder on their faces and exclaiming "happy holi". A group of little girls stop in front of us and paint our faces with colours.

The water bombs and the powder sprays were on us all the time. In the distance I watch monkeys go in and out of the crowd. The already crowded streets were a spectacle with elephants walking through the streets, accompanied by cows.

We stopped in a less crowded area and I was able to taste the famous thandai and Mawa Gujiya, which is a sweet dumpling. I also tried the Ladoos.

After our little snack break, we set off again to continue our walk down the street. Men form groups across the streets and the alcohol seems to be flowing. We continue to receive powders from all sides and we throw them back.

Now that it's the middle of the afternoon, it seems to me that the sun will soon be setting. I have already sprayed people with powder and coloured water.

- There's a party tonight," says Mayra's brother. There will be a race just before. They'll be throwing fluorescent coloured powders this time. It's about two kilometres where the crowd throws the powder at the participants.

- We can go," I asked Gabrielo.

- We're leaving tomorrow morning, Alma," he sighs, running a hand through his hair.

- I swear I'll wake up on time for the start tomorrow," I pleaded. Please, I promise. Gabrielo.

- Before that, let's go home and change.

After a good shower, which reminded me of the kids throwing a bucket of water on us this morning with my belly and thighs coloured orange. I came out clean as a whistle. Gabrielo was waiting for me on the bed looking at the ceiling.

- What's the matter? I asked as I lay down against him.

- Nothing's the matter. It's just that tomorrow is going to be a return to reality. I've changed the flight to an evening one.

- Great, that way I can sleep ! Shall we go?

My darling husband gets up and takes me by the waist as we walk down the stairs. Mayra and her brother are waiting for us in the lobby to leave. We head for the party. The streets have finally started to empty and the crowd is going home. Given the late hour, I'm not surprised.

The music, however, is still playing in some parts of the city. We go to the end of the city to a huge square where a lot of people have gathered. All young people. The lights coming from neon signs hanging everywhere only light up the square slightly.

Everyone is dressed in dark colours, including us. A shot rings out and the race begins. The participants all run around the square while fluorescent powder sprays out from everywhere.

I slather Gabrielo with powder on his face and hair. He grabs my wrist before spilling all the powder from a bag he was holding. My hair gets covered in powder along with part of my face.

Drinks flow through the crowd. I have several drinks with Gabrielo and the music changes. It seems that the race is over. The crowd disperses so they can dance to the beat.

I kiss Gabrielo in the middle of the crowd and a camera flash interrupts us. Mayra holds my phone in her hand and has just taken a picture of us.

-Mayra!

- What? This will be a good souvenir when you get home. Look!She hands me my phone and I admire the picture. I understand why this girl is a photography student now. It's really well taken.

- Yes, you do. Thank you, Madam Mayra.

- You can thank me when I'm a professional. Can I use this photo for my portfolio?

Gabrielo and I glance at each other before turning to her.

- It would be an honour," says Gabrielo.

The party is back in full swing and the crowd grows even larger. A bonfire is burnt and the laughter and cheers increase.

Long live Holi! Happy Holi!

Chapter 14

The worst part after the party is the downhill run. Believe me.

In my desire to party, I overdid it. Mixing alcohol and cannabis was the worst idea of the century. I was so high that I thought my body was going to give out on me. That's when it hit me. Never mix different substances.

I woke up countless times to empty my stomach. And even now that I have nothing left to vomit, I still feel nauseous. I'd better refrain from drinking anything containing cannabis in the future.

And especially not to drink alcohol at the same time.

Gabrielo, well, poor thing. He woke up every time I threw up to see how I was doing. Now that he's finally asleep, I'd rather let him rest. We have a plane to catch tonight at 7pm and we'd better be in shape. He deserves to rest.

I leave the room and go to the living room. Mayra is sitting at the table with her brother. They both look hungover.

- So, you two. How's it going?

- We should ask you," says Mayra. You're white as a corpse.

Her mother approaches her and slaps her on the back of the head. The sound echoes around the room and Mayra is writhing in pain. She grimaces so much that her brother and I burst out laughing despite our headache.

I am shivering despite the temperature of the day. I settle into a seat and take Mayra's jacket.

- Shut up, you'll bring her bad luck," says her mother, glaring at her. Idiot.

She leaves the room and goes upstairs.

- Ouch! She hit me so hard ! As if I didn't have enough of a headache!

- Well done," laughs her brother.

I can see her kicking him through the glass table.

- So, how are you feeling?

- I'll be fine. At least I'm coping with it for now. I feel like I'm greening out and it's horrible.

- We told you not to eat too much of the food there, knowing it was full of drugs," Mayra's brother said.

- Leave me alone. I've learned my lesson now. Could you take me to the bank please, Mayra? I'd like to withdraw some money.

- No problem. Let's go! she exclaims, jumping up from her seat.

We get out to go to the bank. I stop on the way to buy an envelope. I take out the money and put it in an envelope. We stop on the way and I have the envelope wrapped in gift wrap.

On our way back home, I entered our room first. Gabo is still lying on the bed sleeping. I lay down with him before snuggling up to him. Come to think of it, who would have thought that PDA was an offense in this country.

This stay was really a good idea. Especially since the hospitality of Mayra and her family was remarkable. She saved us from a lot of scams and bad behaviour - if we forget yesterday's kiss.

- Alma, get up or we'll miss the plane.

I wake up with a start and sit up hurriedly on the bed. I have a stomach ache in addition to the nausea from this morning.

- It's only 3 p.m.," I said, looking at my watch.

- It it takes at least two hours to get to the airport and to board the plane. Come on, get up Stellina.

- No," I moaned. I'm tired, hungry, sick to my stomach and nauseous. Let me sleep.

I lie down again and feel my body being lifted from the bed. The blanket leaves my body and sleep leaves me. The cool air runs over my skin and I start to shiver again. Gabrielo walks to the door and I ask him to put me down.

- I thought you didn't want to leave. I'll just take you downstairs and ask them to keep you for a while," he says seriously.

- No! I'm going with you. I just wanted to get some more sleep." I mumbled.

- You'll sleep in the car, okay? Go say goodbye to Mayra and the others. I'll be right there.I go downstairs to the living room where

Mayra's family is. I hug Mayra, her mother and her little sister. I shake hands with her father and brother with stinging eyes.

- Take good care of yourself, Alma," Mayra's mother says.

I feel the tears rolling down my cheeks and I do my best to wipe them away. Goodbyes always make me so sad. Mayra's mother takes me in her arms again and wipes away my tears. I thank her for everything and Gabrielo arrives at the same time.

He says goodbye to everyone and we go out to the car. I suddenly remember my gift from this morning. I turn around under the puzzled gaze of everyone. I open the bedside table drawer and take out the package.

- This is for you," I say, handing it to Mayra's mother. I hope you find it useful. Goodbye!

I get into the car and Gabrielo drives off.

- We'll go and see a doctor as soon as we get to New York, okay?

- Why? I asked without understanding.

- You said so yourself. You don't feel well. Not to mention the fact that you're as white as an aspirin tablet. I feel like you're greening out and that worries me. We'll take the jet. Sleep for now, I hope you'll feel better.

- You're always telling me to sleep," I said. Do you want to get rid of me in my sleep?

I squinted at him as he laughed and rolled his eyes.

- Stop with the conspiracy theories. I thought we were supposed to be planning a wedding ceremony?

- Do you feel like it? I asked, suddenly sitting up.

- We'll take care of it when we get there. You'd better get some sleep now.

Before I knew it, we were on the private jet to New York. The flight was uneventful except for my apprehension about ingesting anything. I was so nauseous that just thinking about eating made me feel like I was going to throw up at any moment.

Not to mention my heart pounding and my growing anxiety. I felt like I was going to die because I was so stressed out.

The plane finally lands in New York. We collect our luggage. Gabrielo's driver came to pick us up and I decided to rest for the time of the ride. When I wake up, I am lying in our room. I hear Gabrielo talking to someone outside. Probably the doctor.

I sit up properly on the bed before getting up. I feel slightly dizzy, but decide to go ahead anyway. I go into the bathroom to brush my teeth and take a shower before coming out.

The doctor and Gabrielo are sitting around the bed having what seems to be a very friendly conversation. They turn to me when they hear the bathroom door close. I approach them and greet the doctor.

- Alma, this is my best friend, Cole Jenkins, he's the family doctor. He will be checking you out today.

- Please sit down," he says, pointing to the bed.

I sit down on the bed and Cole begins to examine me. He asks me to call him by his first name. He frowns slightly and takes out his stethoscope. He asks me what's wrong again and widens his eyes as if he's had an idea.

- What have you been doing for the last two days?

- We went out for the evening. And we drank some kind of milk mixed with cannabis," I answer. And alcohol.

- Okay. I think I have my suspicions. Gab comes with me thirty seconds. I have a question to ask you.

He takes my husband aside in the corner of the room. He speaks so softly that I can hardly hear what they say. Cole turns to Gabo one last time and they both return to their seats.

- I have two pieces of good news for you. Maybe three.

- First, I know what Alma has. Secondly, it's nothing serious. Some rest and quiet will only do her good.

- Cole, get to the point.

- I was getting to it. Always so damn impatient! Are you sure you got married on purpose? He asks, turning to me. Because I know a really good lawyer.

I stop myself from laughing at his words.

- And I also know a very good lawyer who can get you fired by tomorrow morning," replies Gabrielo. Cut the crap.

- Fine," exclaims Cole. So, I was saying. Your wife is pregnant. She's feeling bad from all the stuff she's been taking. She's having a green out but she'll be fine by tomorrow morning.

Chapter 15

Pregnant?

"You can already hear the baby's heartbeat," Cole continues. "Gabrielo, sorry, but could you call my assistant and have her fill you in on the paperwork ?" Gabrielo leaves the room quickly and Cole regains his seriousness.

"What are you going to do now?"

"Keep this child. We were planning this anyway." Who would have thought it would happen so soon? I say, dropping onto the bed.

"It's usually a fluke. I can't believe this is how our first meeting happened. How does our mom-to-be feel?"

"Surprised." I think I'm starting to freak out too.

"You're going to be fine. I'm sure you will. You tell Gab to invite me to dinner to celebrate. I want to be the godfather!"

"No problem," I say, laughing.

Cole waves me off and walks out of the room. I lie on the bed still lost in thought. A child. Will I be a good mother? Am I ready to be a mother at all? Gabrielo interrupts my train of thought by entering the room.

"How are you feeling?"

"Much better now that I've slept. What are we going to do?

"That's a good question."

"Well, I'm keeping the baby."

"We're going to get ready for this baby. Wanna have dinner ?"

"I'm starving. I haven't eaten anything since we left."

"I already called the chef. He just finished dinner. Let's go."

We go down to dinner. After we finally finish dinner we go back up to the room to sleep. Gabrielo has just finished his shower and comes out with a towel around his waist.

"Alma, why don't you stop-"

"No," I interrupted him categorically.

"I haven't even finished my sentence," he complains.

"I won't stop working until I have to."

"Alma, be realistic. You're not going to make it through the workload you have. Not to mention the all-nighters you pull before each deadline."

"I can take care of myself. I'll manage somehow. Just trust me."

"Alma, please," Gabo begs with his puppy eyes. "I don't want to pick up your pieces."

"No," I answered hesitantly. "Stop with the look. I won't stop, end of story. I have a big project I've been working on for six months. I can't quit now. Not after all the work I've put in."

"I'm not talking about resigning. I'm talking about slowing down," he huffs.

Gabrielo climbs onto the bed and takes me in his arms. Ah. He must be pouting again. Every time it happens, he reacts the same way. He holds me tightly without saying anything until he falls asleep. Silence is gold, as they say. Except that if it goes on like this, we'll both be sulking.

"Gabrielo?"

No answer. Well, at worst I would have tried to make peace.

"Gabrielo, listen to me. I know you're not sleeping. Let me work. I'm fine."

"I'm just worried. Put yourself in my shoes. I see you running back and forth without a break all week. Not to mention the fact that you're running in stilettos and every time you do I feel like you're going to trip."

"Do I look that unstable in my shoes?"

"No, but the point is. Take care of yourself."

"You always worry too much, I've told you that before. Go to sleep," I said, yawning.

"It's true that you have a bit of a belly now," Gabrielo whispers, feeling my stomach. "I could sleep on it."

"No, you can' t. I've been working out every day. I worked out every day in India."

"It doesn't change the fact that you've gained a belly. I'm sure it's all the food you ate."

"You think? But we ate the same things and you kept your abs," I said, looking at him.

"We ate the same things, but not the same amounts. I'm sure it's the baby taking more space than needed." He laughs before kissing my cheek.

He's touching my sensitivity.

"I swear, if you go on like this, you'll be sleeping on the sofa," I threatened, turning around.

Did I mention that I hate Monday mornings? If I didn't, I do now.

"Rise and shine, Lady Worker. It's time to get up."

The blanket over my body disappears and I feel a cold breeze along my body. I shiver without moving. I curl up in a ball hoping for some warmth.

"I'm cold, Gab, stop."

"It's already 8:34 a.m.," he begins as I stand up abruptly.

"Why didn't you wake me up?"

"Easy, I've been trying to wake you up for an hour. I thought you weren't going to work today at this point."

"No, I am. It's just that I've been sleeping too much lately. Are you going?"

"Yeah, it's about time. I've got an important meeting. I'll see you later," he says, kissing my forehead. "Take care of yourself. The driver will be here in half an hour to pick you up."

I answer him distractedly, still asleep. He lets me go and leaves for work. It's a good thing I start at 10. It's time to get ready. I take a quick shower to wake up and quickly head to the wardrobe. I see my reflection in a mirror and start to inspect myself.

It's true that I've put on weight. I run my hand over my belly and lightly caress it. I am pregnant. I still can't believe it.

Anyway, I really need to get dressed. What am I going to wear today? I really hate that moment before I go out when I can't decide what to wear.

My stilettos are winking at me from the back of the room. I might not wear them for a while. I might as well enjoy them. Even if it's just for today. I'd better hurry before I'm late.

I'm on my way downstairs when the housekeeper - Gabrielo has decided to take over the one from his childhood home to 'make my life easier' - stops me on my way.

"You should eat something before you leave, madam."

"Call me Alma and stop being so formal," I say, smiling.

"Very good, Alma. Now let's eat. Gabrielo took care to ask the chef to prepare breakfast for you. He also told me not to let you go out on an empty stomach."

Gabrielo and his instructions... I go into the dining room and have a cup of tea with cookies before going out. When I get to the office, Jayna is already waiting for me to start.

"How was the honeymoon?"

"Unforgettable. I tried everything I could get my hands on," I reply, sitting down at my desk. "So, what are the appointments?"

"From 2 to 6 p.m., near the rose garden. For now, there are some alterations to be made. We have to leave in ten minutes."

"We're still doing that? I thought we were done with this", I sighed.

"The bride doesn't fit into the dress and the ceremony starts in an hour. We have to hurry to the ceremony site."

"Let's go. Bring a corset with you. We may not be able to do all the touch-ups."

That's why I'm asking brides to watch their weight gain. Oh, dear. I hate these things. We hurriedly got into the car and drove off. The bride is already waiting for us in her room.

"Thank God you're here in time!"

"Put the dress on so I can see what the problem is," I ordered, opening my briefcase.

The bride put on the dress and I watched her do it in silence. My goodness, that's more than a few grams she's gained. She's definitely gained three centimetres around her waist. I ask Jayna to get the corset out so the bride can put it on.

I zip up the dress, keeping my fingers crossed. I've made a few small alterations and the corset should make things easier. Bingo! The dress zips up without a problem. The bride thanks us and we head back to the office.

"It's already time for lunch," says Jayna. "Let's go and eat outside."

"No problem, let's go. I'm starving." We stop at a restaurant near the company to eat. Our orders soon arrive and we can finally eat.

"Alma, when are you going to hold a wedding ceremony and introduce us to your husband?"

"Not anytime soon. I have to attend my sister's wedding in a few weeks. I'll have to go away for a while again."

"I feel sorry for you. Your sister is really not a gift."

"I know," I sighed, "but I don't have that much choice."

I feel dizzy and close my eyes, taking a deep breath. The fatigue is starting to kick in. I knew I should have slept some more.

"Are you OK?" Jayna worries.

"I'm fine," I smiled, pinching the bridge of my nose. "Just a bit tired from being back at work. We'd better get going, don't you think?"

"Yes, we should. Let's go before it's too late."

My phone rings, Gabrielo's name pops up. I get into the passenger seat and try to answer it. My phone slips out of my hand and I feel the fatigue take over.

Chapter 16

"Alma! Alma!"

I feel something against my cheek. Jayna's voice echoes in my head without stopping.

"Stop screaming, Jay."

I open my eyes and meet a blue-green gaze. It's weird, Jayna has brown eyes. I frown and concentrate. Jayna is on my left and has a worried look on her face. Gabrielo's face then enters my field of vision.

"Gab?" I muttered, still in a daze. "What are you doing here?"

"Grazie al cielo," Gabrielo exclaims, squeezing my hand. "You scared me."

He holds me tightly and I return his embrace. I sit up on the bed and observe my surroundings. I feel as if I have been drained of all my strength. It's awful.

"Where are we?"

"In the hospital, Tesoro. You passed out in your colleague's car. How are you feeling?"

"Tired," I said, leaning against him. "I want to go home."

"We'll go home soon, just rest for now."

The smile on Gabrielo's face becomes increasingly blurred and I feel myself sinking again. Then I woke up on our bed at home. The room was empty and it seems to be the middle of the afternoon. I'm in my pyjamas. Weird. I walk down the stairs and hear voices coming from the living room.

Gabrielo is talking on the phone with the speaker on. I watch him from a distance, waiting for him to finish talking. When he finishes his call, I approach him and he turns to me. He beckons me to approach him. I step forward hesitantly and he sits me on his lap.

"We should have a chat," Gabrielo suggests, grabbing my chin and lifting my head.

"If that's the way it's going to be, I'd rather you yell at me once and for all."

"I won't," Gabrielo replies calmly, "otherwise your conscience will be clear. Now tell me: what is the problem here?"

I remain silent, my head down. Gabrielo gives me an tired look and sighs before he lets himself go against the sofa. He looks exhausted. I can tell by the way his hair is messed up from the amount of times he's run his hand through it. He looks exhausted and it's very much my fault.

"I was wrong and you were right, Gabrielo. I should have taken it easy like you asked me to this morning."

There is a silence in the room and I feel uncomfortable. Okay, I was wrong and I should have listened to him, but he could react to my apology. My conscience is heavy and it's deserved.

"It's lovely of you to admit your mistakes," my husband replies, putting his head on my neck. "You're going to have a lot of free time for the rest of the week. And the next nine months for that matter."

"Sorry?"

"Game over, sweetheart. You're staying home," he said, planting a kiss on my cheek. "I gave you a chance and you blew it, you should have been more careful."

"Gabrielo, please. Come on, you have to be joking."

"Too late. The doctor said you need to calm down, rest and avoid unnecessary stress. That's what you'll get, peace, rest and no stress. Do you want to miscarry?"

"No!" I said, feeling my pulse quicken.

"Then you'll stay here. If you want to work, you can do it from here, but this back and forth stuff stops now. Is that clear?"

"Yes," I sighed, keeping my head down.

"Call Meavy or whoever you want to come and keep you company. I've got to go. I'll see you tonight. Don't forget to eat what the housekeeper cooked."

He kisses me one last time before getting up and walking out of the room. I am speechless. This is the first time Gabrielo has been so angry. He won't give in this time. Too bad. It was in vain but I tried.

There is nothing I can do. Meavy is working, Jayna is working, everybody is working but me. I might as well get some fresh air. I've already eaten what Mrs Warrens made for me and I'm not hungry anymore. I'm going to visit Meavy at her company. The last time I spoke to her was yesterday and I still haven't told her the good news. I get in my car and call Jayna on the way.

"Alma, how are you feeling?" Jayna asks quickly.

"I'm fine, don't worry. Do me a favour and bring me the two dresses I was working on at home. I already texted you the address."

"No problem, boss. You should really get some rest. The CEO was worried sick when I picked up your phone to tell him we were in the hospital. It was cute. Congratulations, by the way.""I'm sorry about that and thank you," I said, laughing. "At least you've met my husband."

"I was in shock when I saw him walk into the room. You scored big by marrying the new bachelor that everyone was raving about."

"I know, I know. That's what we call being lucky. He's not single anymore."

"Share some of your luck with me if that's how it is. I need it too."

"Don't worry. Everything comes at a time."

Our conversation continues until I find myself in front of Meavy's office. I knock on the door and enter the room. No one is there. That's strange. She should be here now.

I sit in her seat waiting for her to come back. I hope she's quick, I wanted to surprise her. My phone rings in my pocket and my husband's name comes up. I put the phone down on the desk without bothering to answer. I get three more calls and finally decide to answer.

"Hello?"

"Alma, where are you?" Gabrielo asks impatiently.

"I'm outside. Why?"

"Alma, please come home."

"I'll be home in a few hours."

"Do you know how worried I was when your secretary answered the phone and told me you were in hospital? I thought I was losing it. I wouldn't be able to forgive myself if anything happened to you. I could have stopped you but I didn't."

"I'm sorry about that. I really am. I knew you were right but I wanted to prove you wrong."

I hear him sigh on the other end of the phone. He's got a point. I should have been careful and listened to him this morning. It's my fault and playing with his nerves won't help the situation.

"I've gone to see Meavy," I sighed. "I'll be back soon. Is that ok ?"

"Okay. Text me and I'll come get you."

"I'll see you later. Bye."

I hang up and sigh one last time. I should have been more careful. The past is gone and rehashing it won't change anything. The office door finally opens and I'm about to call Meavy before I realise she's not alone.

And that her mouth is full. Great.

Thank you all for reading my story!

Please comment and vote!

Chapter 17

Meavy is carried to the sofa by her... Boyfriend? Booty call? No idea. Things are starting to go a little too far for my taste. I clear my throat and they stop moving in a hurry.

Sorry lovebirds, but not in front of me. Meavy immediately stands up with her lipstick scattered around her mouth.

" Alma, since when did...?"

"I've been here? At least twenty minutes. And this is?"

"Er... . Alma, this is Liam. Liam, my best friend Alma."

He holds out his hand to me, smiling. I'd rather not take it after I've seen where it was just a minute ago.

"Nice to meet you," I say, putting a fake smile on my face.

"Likewise," he replies embarrassed.

"Can I borrow Meavy for a few minutes?"

"No problem," he says, walking out. "I've got work to do, so I'll see you later, Meavy."

The door closes behind him and Meavy sits down in front of her desk. I take my place - hers, at last - and stare at her.

"Who? How? And where?"

"Liam Narsher. He's a teacher at the university. We met during my internship. He's the one who validated my degree."

"A professor, huh? How old is he to teach at the university?"

"He's 28. Believe me, once he takes his shirt off, he turns heads. I was gonna tell you about it on our Friday night out. What are you doing here by the way?"

"Sit down, I've got some good news for you."

"We're going to live a lavish life and go to England?"

"No! Why England?"

"It's where the queen is and I've always live there for a while. And I met amazing men there," she says as I sigh.

"I thought you were with your teacher. Besides, I'm married and my husband suits me very well."

"One of us has to keep an open mind. Have options. Especially when I'm not married."

"You really never stop," I chuckled.

"I love you too," she says with her hand on her heart. "So, about that good news?"

"I'm coming to that. I want to take a picture first."

"Let's do it," Meavy says, touching herself up.

She positions herself while I pull out my phone. I smile and activate the video.

"Say 'Alma's pregnant!'", I say with a smile.

Meavy stops smiling and looks stunned. I burst out laughing and turn to her while she freezes.

"No!" she shouts. "You're kidding!"

I already know which way this announcement is going. I nod as Meavy continues to deny it.

"I mean... Why? How? No, you're not!" she shouts in panic.

"Meav', I'm pregnant," I laughed.

"I won't fall for the same trick again."

Okay, this is deserved after the bad joke I played on her a few months ago. I knew it was going to come back to me.

"I swear to God, it's true."

A shrill scream echoes through the room before Meavy picks me up and starts jumping up and down. She holds me in her arms as she jumps and I join her.

"I'm going to be an auntie! I want to be the godmother!"

"What is it with you all wanting to be godparents?"

"Who asked before me?" Meavy replies on guard. "I'll get rid of them."

"Gabrielo's best friend," I laugh at her reaction.

My phone vibrates on the desk. Gabrielo has come to pick me up. Two hours have already passed since I got here. Meavy is still in her world about the baby. I greet her and go out to the lift. Gabrielo is waiting for me in front of the building to go home.

"So ?"

"So what?" I asked, frowning.

"Have you finally accepted your situation?"

"I've accepted it from the start. It's just that I'm having trouble getting used to it. All of a sudden I find out I'm pregnant. I've just started working and I have to stop. I've made so many sacrifices to get to this point that it hurts," I admitted, feeling tears about to break out.

"Alma. . ."

"I know. It's for the baby's sake and mine. I'm just having a little trouble swallowing it all."

"It'll pass," he says, stroking my cheek with his thumb.

"Your mother is inviting us to her house for dinner next week," I say, remembering our discussion. "We can tell her about the baby."

"That would be nice. She'd told me about it. You can meet the rest of my family."

"I'm looking forward to it," I replied, resting my head on his shoulder.

The only detail Gabrielo had left out of the story was that there was a charity dinner for the orphanage two days later. I had to get ready at the last minute to make sure we were on time. Once we got out of the limousine, we headed into the hall.

The reception room was already full of people drinking and talking. Gabrielo took me to greet various acquaintances with him. I forced my smile so much that my cheeks hurt. The children from the orphanage are in a room upstairs playing with each other from what I hear.

Gabrielo let me rest for a few minutes while he went to talk to other people. I'm already exhausted from being here and bored. I go upstairs to sit in the quiet. The children are in a hidden room at the end of the corridor. I enter the room after knocking.

"Hi, do you mind if I sit here?"

The children shake their heads and I sit on the floor in the corner of the room. I take off my heels, which seem to hurt my feet more than anything else. Pumps really can be instruments of torture sometimes.

One of the younger children walks over to me with a book in his hand.- Shall I read it to you?

He nods and hands me the book. He moves a little closer to me and sits down abruptly on my lap.

"Slowly, with my belly, please," I ask, smiling at him.

"Boo boo in your tummy ?" He asked in his small voice.

He raises his hand and touches my belly. He immediately raises his head to see my reaction. He then puts his head on my belly and kisses it.

"I kissed the boo boo better," he smiles before sitting back down on my lap.

Oww. I'm going to kidnap this kid.

He's so cute. I give him a kiss on the cheek before answering him. I want to adopt him but I don't think Gabrielo will agree. Even more so now that I have to rest.

"No, but there's a baby inside. You have to be careful so that it grows as big as you do."

He frowns and touches my stomach again. It's true that it's a bit more visible now. Even through my dress you can see my belly forming. I put Max - that's his name - back on my lap properly and start to read him his story.

Other children join in the storytelling. The story of the 1001 Nights seems to interest a lot of children, even the older ones. I finish the story of Sinbad the sailor and everyone starts asking questions. Max thanks me and gives me a hug. He then gets off my lap and goes off to play with the other children.

"This is where you were," a voice whispers against my ear.

"Gabrielo!" I exclaimed, startled. "You scared me."

"Sorry, sorry," he laughed, intertwining our fingers.

He plays with my wedding ring, watching me.

"There's someone I'd like you to meet downstairs. Let's go."

"Gabrielo, I want to take a child with me", I asked in a soft voice.

"First of all, I hope you meant to adopt because we're not stealing a child tonight. Also, why?"

"He's so cute," I countered, pouting. "Come on, please."

He sighs before putting his arm around my waist.

"We'll talk about it tonight."

I slip on my stilettos and lose my balance as I walk. Gabrielo barely catches me and puts his hand around my waist.

"You'll have to change your heels, Alma. You'll be crushed like a pancake otherwise."

"Ah, ah, ah. Thanks, Sherlock. I've hardly got anything else in my dressing room. I need to go shopping for a reasonable height and stop wearing stilettos. My back's bad enough as it is."

"We'll stop before dinner at my parents' tomorrow," Gabo suggests. "For now, we have to go downstairs and join the others."

I wrap my arm around his and we go downstairs. The gala has officially started and everyone seems to be enjoying the food and drinks and chatting. We approach a woman dressed in a stunning salmon coloured dress. Even though she is from the back, you can tell that she looks good. A man approaches her and kisses her briefly.

"Steven", Gabrielo calls as the man in front of us turns around. "So you don't greet me anymore."

"Gab, I haven't seen you for six months," he exclaims with a smile, taking my husband in his arms before turning to me. "Who's this?"

"My wife, Alma," he replies, smiling and taking me by the waist. "Alma, this is Steven Clarks, my childhood friend. He's working as a sommelier in some major hotels at the moment."

"Pleased to meet you," I say, shaking his hand.

The young woman next to him finally turns towards us. I recognise her face immediately and we jump into each other's arms. We continue to exchange hugs until Gabrielo grabs me by the waist and pulls me towards him.

"What are you doing to my corazón?" the woman exclaims as she takes me back into her arms.

Chapter 18

"Your... corazón?" Gabrielo repeats, raising his eyebrows and looking in my direction.

I pretend to look behind me for a moment. My glance goes from him to behind me a second time before I point out myself.

"Yes, you," Gabrielo retorts with a sneer. "Stop pretending, you heard me right."

I take my friend in my arms while raising the eyebrows.

"And why not?"

"Because she's my fiancée," Steven says. "And I didn't know I had to be wary of the women around her too."

"Neither did I," my husband agrees. "Meavy is definitely the one to watch out for right now."

They both look at us sideways before giving each other a confused look. We glance at each other before bursting into laughter.

"Sorry, but it was too tempting", Amber exclaims. "You didn't tell me you got married, Alma."

"And you that you were engaged", I retorted. "Everything happened quickly, so I didn't have much time."

"My parents still don't know that I'm back in New York," Amber says. "I was going to announce it right before Mila's wedding."

We continue our discussion while heading towards the sofas in the middle of the room.

"Girls", Gabrielo and Steve interrupt, "we would like an explanation."

"Alma," says Amber, pointing to me, "my cousin. Not my ex. Where was I?"

We continue to discuss until I start to yawn. Gabrielo glances at me out of the corner of his eye and I discreetly shake my head. I don't want to go home yet.

"So, your family?" Amber asks.

"We still get on so well. I am still going to Mila's wedding."

"I feel sorry for us for having to go to that ungrateful thing's wedding. After all you've done for her, the one thing she saw fit to do was steal your boyfriend."

"Amber, it's okay. I'm over it. Even more so now that I'm married and pregnant. Trust me on that."

"Pregnant?" She says with a frown.

Her gaze moves from me to my belly without stopping. She holds up a finger in my direction and places it on my belly, applying a little pressure.

"For real?" she asks.

"For real."

"And you're planning to travel to Spain like this?"

"The gynecologist told me it's okay. We'll check again before we leave."

"We'd better go," Gabrielo says, coming up behind me. "It is already 11 pm and we have things to do tomorrow."

I wave to Amber and Steven before going out to go back home. The journey is quiet and comfortable while I close the eyes some seconds. I feel the smell of Gabo near me and open my eyes. He smiles at me as he meets my gaze and continues to walk.

"Go back to sleep, sleeping beauty."

I don't answer anything and just observe him, my head resting against his chest. He takes me to our room and puts me on the bed. I remove my stilettos and remove my make-up quickly. This evening will have exhausted me. I hear the sound of water running in the bathtub and enter the bathroom.

"Stellina, you want to take a shower?"

I nod, now fully awake. We both get into the bath and I throw a bath bomb inside. Gabrielo takes me in his arms and lets me go against his chest. I feel his hand go down my body and stop on my belly. He lays kisses along my face and in the hollow of my neck.

I hold myself against him, enjoying his touch. I make a half turn on myself to face him. I kiss him and he hugs me. I deepen our kiss and rest my forehead on his.

In the shower, in the bath, on the bed. I think after that, I won't move for the next two weeks. Okay, I may be exaggerating a bit.

Gabrielo is sleeping peacefully next to me on his stomach. He's really adorable when you see him like that. I run a hand through his hair before sitting on the bed.

It is 11:45 am. I rub my eyes when I see what time it is. We are late! I shake Gabrielo vigorously and he gets up with a jolt.

" What is it?" He growls while lying down again.

"Get up, we are going to be late for the lunch with your parents", I say while getting up.

He grabs me by the waist and pulls me on the bed against him. I shake him off and release myself from his embrace. I take a quick shower and head to the dressing room. Gabrielo walks in five minutes later and grabs a pair of jeans and a shirt.

I think it's the first time I've seen him wearing jeans. He's always dressed up to go to work. Even when we were in India, he refused to wear jeans even when I got rid of the rest of his wardrobe.

"What's the matter?" He asks with a smile. "I know you like to look at me, but you better hurry up before we're even more late."

"Whose fault is that, huh? I told you we'd better get some sleep early."

"Be honest, you're the one who asked for more," he said, pressing my back against his chest. "You even begged."

He kisses the back of my neck a few times and places his chin on the top of my head. His arms wrap around my belly and begin to caress it.

"You should think about getting a new wardrobe", he says thoughtfully. "No heels today while I think about it."

"Think well because I am going to wear them."

"Alma", Gabrielo growls while tightening his hands against me.

"I don't have anything else", I exclaimed turning to him. "I'm going to wear lower square heels so it's okay."

"If you say so. We'll go sneaker shopping after lunch with my mom."

"No problem. Now let me get dressed. I need to look decent."

He leaves the room in a hurry and I watch him without saying anything. I hurriedly put on a simple skirt and a top. It's getting hot and I want to feel comfortable.

I take one last look at myself in the car before I get out. Everything is going to be fine. I turn to Gabrielo at the wheel.

"What about the adoption?" I asked. "I was serious. I fell asleep so we couldn't talk about it last night."

"You really want to adopt this little boy ? I have nothing against the idea. It's just that it's a huge responsibility. If you feel like you're ready to take it, then go ahead. I'm with you."

" Seriously? I thought you'd say no so I could get some rest."

"I know staying home when everyone else is doing something is frustrating. You've been doing it for almost a week and it's really not for you. You look unhappy."

"So, can I go back to work?"

"Still no", he counters, "but nice try. I wanted to tell you that this child could brighten up the day. But I want you to think about it calmly and give me an answer in a few days."

"What if he gets adopted by then?"

"Trust me on that. Just think about it and I'll take care of the rest."

The car stops and crosses a small alley before a huge building enters my field of vision. A rush of stress takes me and Gabrielo takes my hand.

"Relax", Gabrielo murmurs, taking me by the waist. "That will do you only good. You are not not going to get eaten and I am with you."

I nod before he opens the door and enters the place.

Chapter 19

Rosaria welcomes us with open arms and I hand her the bottle of champagne I brought with us. She takes me in her arms and thanks me saying that I should not have bothered. We continue our way to the garden where our lunch will take place.

The barbecue is already set up and a young man is busy with the grill. Gabrielo hides me behind him and heads for the barbecue.

"So, Alex, did you miss me?" He asks by tapping him on the shoulder which makes his brother jump.

"Not at all. I saw you two weeks ago. The only person I wanted to see was your wife."

"I guess it's good timing, since I came," I say, stepping to my husband's side.

Alex is about to take me in his arms when Gabrielo stops him. He slaps his hand and puts his arms around me, making me step back.

"What are you doing?" I asked, backing away in spite of myself.

"Go and touch other people's wives if you want, but not mine", Gabrielo announced, glaring at him.

"Gabrielo, it is your brother. He is not going to do anything strange", I sighed while looking at him.

"It is what said Guiseppe's wife before he slapped her a butt", he argues while looking at him.

"You're the one who paid me to do it!" Alex exclaims, looking outraged. "And I was 9 !""The fact is that you did it anyway!"

"You're both weird."

I step away from Gabrielo and head to the kitchen where his mother is. I walk into the kitchen and find Rosaria cooking with a little boy.

"He's so cute!" I exclaimed when I saw him.

"Good, he's your nephew. Would you mind taking care of him for a while? He never stops tasting everything he finds," my mother-in-law complained. "If this keeps up, lunch will be gone before it even starts.""That's not true!" The little boy says as he picks up a piece of meat. "I'm helping you check if it's good."

I laugh and then come over and take my nephew in my arms. He stares at me blankly before grabbing a lock of my hair.

"What's your name champion?"

"I'm Luca," he replies, playing with my hair. "And you, what's your name?"

"Alma," I said, smiling at him. "Luca, do you want to help me do a surprise for grandma ?"

"Surprise?" He repeats while clapping his hands. "Yes !"

I whisper in his ear my plan for later and he nods without hesitation. We smile at each other before going to play in the garden.

Alex and Gabrielo seem to have finally finished arguing and talk like civilized people. I approach them with Luca in my arms.

"Luca!" Gabo exclaims when he sees the child in my arms. "How are you doing, buddy?"

He lifts him up and Luca starts to laugh out loud. They both leave to play in a corner of the garden and I sit down to breathe. I have a feeling this day is going to go well.

"So, Dear Sister-in-law, what do you think of my brother?" Alex asks as he sits down next to me.

"Honestly?"

He nods with a smile.

"I love him even if he acts weird sometimes," I said. "I mean, why does he walk around naked in the house whenever he feels like it ?"

Alex burst out laughing and looked at me without stopping to smile.

"I didn't expect this," he says, looking at me. "He's got himself quite a wife. I can't wait to see you guys be parents."

"Me too," I said, thinking.

"We said that we would talk to her together, Alexandro," a deep voice exclaims behind me.

"That's right," a more delicate voice adds.

I turn and see two men and a woman coming towards us. One looks like Gabrielo except for his eyes which are completely green and the other, his father, is just like him. The young woman is a spitting image of Rosaria.

"Hello," I said, smiling nervously.

"Hi, I'm Guiseppe, the older brother of the weirdo behind you," he said, holding out his hand.

Alex puts a hand on his heart with a shocked face before taking my hand and looking into mine.

"I am Gabrielo's father but we've met before for work," the older man says, ignoring his son, "Call me Francesco. I hope my son didn't cause you too much trouble."

"Not at all", I said, laughing. "I'm the one who worries him all the time. Let's keep it between us, but I think he would rather have me as a housewife."

Francesco laughed at my words and patted me on the shoulder.

"It's true that he used to say that when he was younger. He wanted his wife to stay at home and not have to take care of anything but himself. That brat!"

"I thought he was sexist back then," the young woman laughed. "I'm Bella, the oldest of all these siblings."

I smile at her while Francesco watches Alex on my left.

"In the meantime, that brat remains your son", Gabrielo retorts while arriving behind me. "Are they badmouthing me?"

"Not really," I answer while holding him by the arm.

"Come and eat! It is ready!" Gabrielo's mother shouts from the other end of the garden.

She is with Kayla, Luca's mother. I met her during my little break in the kitchen to help out earlier. She is absolutely adorable. A sweetheart. We sit down at the table and Luca sits next to me.

As the meal comes to an end, he tugs on my sleeve to get my attention.

"What is it, Luca?"

"The surprise," he whispers, looking at me.

"I completely forgot, thank you," I say, giving him a kiss on the cheek. "Gabrielo, can you give me the car keys, I forgot something inside."

"I'm coming," Luca says, jumping out of his seat and taking my hand.

Kayla waves me over and I smile at her. We go to the car and I pick up two different boxes. I give the smaller one to Luca and carry the larger one. I bend down to his level to give him my instructions.

"When we get there, you're going to give the box to Grandma and Grandpa after I put the big box on the table, okay?"

"Okay!"

I take his hand again and we head towards the rest of the family.

"What did you bring us?" Rosaria asks with a frown.

"A present," I say, taking my seat.

Luca rushes over to her and hands her the small box. Rosaria opens the big box and finds the cake inside.

"Did you make it?" Alexandro asks without taking his eyes off the cake.

"I did," I answer, putting my head on Gabrielo's shoulder.

"So that's what you were doing this morning in the kitchen. You should have asked the chef."

"Stop it with that. I can do that much."

I watch Rosaria open the box Luca gave her a few moments earlier. She gets up and drops her chair on the floor.

"Gabrielo is going to have a child," she shouts, coming to hug me.

I return her embrace smiling. Gabrielo looks at me surprised by my announcement. I make him a wink and he smiles at me. After receiving congratulations from everyone, we start cutting the cake. Luca makes his way through the world behind me and grabs my leg.

"I want cake first", he demands, looking me in the eye. "The others, they didn't do anything but I worked, I deserve more. Please!"

"Right away," I replied, giving him some cake.

Ah, children.

Chapter 20

The time to leave has come. Three weeks have passed since the lunch at Gabrielo's house. I made the decision to adopt Max against all expectations. We'll wait until the end of the school year to do it. At least, that's the plan so we don't rush him too much.

He knows that he is going to be adopted and we come to visit him three times a week so that he is used to see us. Gabrielo has even become more attached to him than he originally thought.

Our bags are ready and we are going to take the plane with Steven and Amber. I am just 4 months pregnant and everything is going well, except for the 2 kilos I have gained recently.

My belly is much more apparent and we came to an agreement with Gabrielo that I would no longer wear heels over 2 inches. Following our appointment with the obstetrician, we decided to wait to find out the sex of the baby.

For now, we are going to Spain for my sister's wedding.I take my seat next to Gabrielo, Amber and Steven are sitting behind us. The jet takes off and I start to fall asleep. This pregnancy makes me much more tired than I would have imagined. I mean, I'm usually tired so I probably shouldn't complain too much. I even agreed to take the private jet for this reason.

When I wake up, Gabrielo has been replaced by Amber. I frown as I catch sight of her and look around. Where is he?

"He's in the back talking with Steven in the back room. They didn't want to wake you up."

"When are we getting there?" I asked as I lay back on her lap.

"Less than an hour. How are you feeling?"

"As nervous as you," I answered without looking at her. "I want to turn back."

"Me too," Amber said, caressing my head on her lap. "They opened the family house to gather us all together. It wasn't enough to come all the way from New York, we have to support them all at the same time. "

"I chuckle at her remark but can't help but agree with her. Our stay will be quite long. Amber makes a quick call and we resume our conversation. The pilot announces that we will be landing soon so I buckle up.

When we leave the plane, a driver is already waiting for us in a car. We give him the instructions to reach the family residence. The car parks in front of the gate and I get out of the car with Amber.

"We are going to enter first to say hello, wait for us here", Amber orders by taking me by the hand. When we get inside the residence, we throw each other a nervous look.

"We are in deep shit", I sighed.

"Speak for yourself, Mrs. Moretti. I'll have time to make something up before we get there, not you. Anyone can see you're pregnant from three miles away."

"Weren't you supposed to reassure me?"

"Not when I'm in trouble with you."

"Anyway, I'll just go to my room and come back."

We enter the mansion and go upstairs. Just before we hit the hallway, I hear my mom calling my name. I turn to her with Amber and she widens her eyes.

"¡Oh Dios Mio!" she says when she sees me, which makes me roll my eyes.

"Good to see you too mom", I say sarcastically with a fake smile plastered on my face.

"Don't tell me that you will come to your sister's wedding like that?" she exclaims, grabbing my shoulder.

"I'm not due for at least five months," I began, pulling her hands away, "so yes."

"Who is the father?"

"A man," I described, smiling at her. "We're going to have to go if you don't have anything else to say."

I turn around and continue my way through the hallways. If I remember correctly, his room should be around here.

"Where are we going?" Amber asks behind me.

"To see Yuma. I'd rather tell him than have him find out on his own."

"I had forgotten about him. How has he been since the last time?"

"He's doing great. He even has a girlfriend from what I heard."

I knock on the door and enter the room. He is there as usual, smoking at the window. I slowly walk over before I hug him in surprise.

"Yuma!"

"I told you to stop doing that," he laughs.

"And I told you to quit smoking. I guess we can't have everything we want in life."

"That's true," he admits, pulling me into a hug. "Is it me or have you gotten fatter?"

I hit him on the shoulder while Amber bursts out laughing.

"Dare tell me I'm fat again and you will not see my offspring."

"Always the big words with you, it's not like you're-"

He looks down at me and sees my stomach. He touches it carefully and looks up at me.

"Who is the father?" he asks with a serious look.

"My husband," I smile nervously. " 'You can't start the next chapter of your life if you keep rereading the last one.' That's what you told me, right? I decided to take your advice for once."

"I am speechless. Why wasn't I invited to the wedding? Let alone notified?"

"Because there hasn't been a ceremony yet. We'll do that later. I had a hard time juggling everything after the wedding registration. I'd like you to meet my husband. He's waiting out in the front with Amber's fiancé.""Seriously Alma, don't tell me you married the first guy you saw to get over James," he grunts as he puts down his cigarette pack.

How did he know?

"It's a little more complicated than that. Besides, I'm serious, quit smoking. What am I going to do if something happens to you? I don't want to be the one you leave behind."

"Stop talking like that. I'm not leaving you alone anytime soon. I plan on pestering you for a lot longer."

"Don't you want to grow up for once?" I laughed.

"Not with you. I'd rather be myself," he said with a smile. "Now it's about time I go see your husband."

Yuma stands up and walks out of the room. I speed up to catch up with him and start trotting behind him.

"Yuma! Wait for me!"

He finally stops and waits for us in front of the stairs. I hold on to the railing, catching my breath as best I can. Since I stopped working out, nothing is going well and being pregnant doesn't help. I should have trusted my instincts and continued if Gabrielo hadn't stopped me. I've become a slacker now.

We cross the rest of the residence and arrive at the gate.

"You guys took a long time," Gabrielo exclaims, getting out of the car to give me a hug. "Is everything okay?"

"Just fine," I replied, smiling at him. "I have someone special to introduce you to. Come out of hiding."

Yuma came out from behind a pillar and walked towards us. He looks at us blankly and seems to be waiting for me to introduce him.

"This is Yuma, my twin brother. Yuma, this is my husband, Gabrielo."

They challenge each other with their eyes and shake hands. The atmosphere is tense. Eventually they start talking and I go to the trunk to help get our luggage out. Just as I'm about to lift a suitcase, arms grab it before me.

"How many times do I have to tell you not to carry those suitcases?" Gabrielo sighs, judging me with his eyes. "They weigh a ton and the doctor warned you against carrying too much weight. It's not good for your back."

"It's not that heavy," I grumbled. "You can't carry it all by yourself. I'll just roll it."

"Alma, please," Gabo whispered in my ear, "we had an agreement."

"Very well," I say, raising my hands. "I won't touch it anymore."

"Thank you," he says while kissing me on the cheek.

He grins at me and takes out the rest of our stuff. Yuma smiles as he watches us. This is a good sign. Now we just need to meet the head of the house. That is, my grandmother.

Chapter 21

I enter the room of my grandmother, hand in hand with Gabrielo. She stares at me from a distance without saying anything. I always hated it when she kept silent like that since I was a child. It was her way of keeping her thoughts to herself without flinching. She seems to be thinking and gets up from her chair.

- Alma, cariño," she says, taking me in her arms. You are bringing me a surprise with you now.

She moves away a little to be able to admire me completely. She gently runs a hand over my belly, smiling. Then, she turns to Gabo who seems to me stiff as a board. She looks him up and down without speaking.

- Can I know who you are? She asks sharply.

I thought we had agreed that she would greet him warmly. Not like he was an intruder in her house.

If that's being warm, I can't imagine what she'd say if she was cold.

- Gabrielo Moretti, your granddaughter's husband," he replies, recovering his composure.

- I don't think I gave you my granddaughter's hand, young man," my grandmother counters without blinking.

- Grandma, please," I pleaded, grabbing her arm.

She moves away from him and goes to take a glass of wine in her hands. She puts it back down without touching it and asks me to sit in the chair where she had been a few moments earlier. Then she turns around and stands in front of Gabrielo.

- I have something to ask you. What will you do if you lose this child? I believe that this is the only thing that brings you together.

- Alma remains my wife no matter what. Our marriage is a promise to keep loving each other even when it's hard, because Alma is worth it. No matter what happens, I will be there to support her.

This touches my heart. I feel tears forming in my eyes. Damn hormones. I wipe my tears away as quietly as I can, keeping myself from sniffling. My grandmother stands in front of me and holds my hands in hers.

- I'm glad you have someone to count on," my grandmother says. Your grandfather would be so relieved.

- Thank you, Grandma," I said, sniffling.

- I'm sure you'll make an amazing mother. Just look up and be proud of everything you've been through to get here.

I hug my grandmother before bursting into tears. She's the only person I have left here with Yuma. She has looked after me and Yuma all these years. I don't know what I would do without her.

- Welcome back to Spain," she murmured in Spanish, rubbing my back. As for you, Gabrielo, welcome into our family. Take care of Alma for me.

- Don't worry, ma'am.

- Call me Nadia. For now, go and rest. Alma will need it, especially with dinner coming up. Dinner will be served soon. I will see you then.

We went back upstairs to my room to rest. I let myself down on the bed and Gabrielo joins me.

- Quite a family, huh?

- You said it," he replies, resting my head on his chest in a hug. I haven't even met your parents yet.

- I'm not looking forward to seeing them at all," I say, returning his hug. My grandmother makes all the decisions around here. She's the boss.

- Well, that's an incredible grandma you have there.

- I know," I said, closing my eyes against his chest. I'm lucky to have her. And I'm lucky to have you too.

I feel lips resting against my forehead and I relax even more. This encounter has been intense. I hear footsteps coming down the stairs and voices heading downstairs.

- It's time for dinner," I say with a sigh.

We get out of bed and I lead us into the dining room. Almost everyone was settled when we entered and eyes turned to us. Amber waved at me from across the table and I came to sit next to her.

- Who is missing? I asked through the hubbub of the room.

- Mila and her fiancée," Amber answered without taking her eyes off the door. Your parents, mine and grandma.

- They should be here soon then.

Speaking of the devil, here he is pointing the end of its tail. Mila, come into the room with James and my parents. I tense up helplessly. Although two years have passed without me seeing her, I really haven't missed her. I would go back to New York if it weren't for Grandma.

Gabrielo takes my hand and intertwines our fingers. He strokes the top of my hand and looks at me with concern. I reassure him before turning my attention back to my parents. They stare at us from across the table. I do my best to ignore them. Grandma enters the room and the meal begins.

Yuma is deep in conversation with Steven and Gabrielo about liquor and anecdotes I've lost track of. They seem to get along great with each other. Amber chats with me throughout the meal and we both try to forget about the presence of our family members.

The rest of the family eventually left the table and only my grandmother, my parents, Gabrielo, Mila, James and I remained. As I left, Amber gave me a little "good luck". I got up to leave the table when my mother called out to me.

- Sit down, we need to talk.

- I'm fine, thanks. I haven't had a real conversation with you in two years and I'm just fine.

- Alma, let's hear what she has to say," my grandmother suggests.

I sit back down in my seat and wait for her to start talking. Gabrielo puts a hand around my waist and pulls me onto his lap. I ask him to let me sit in my chair, but he turns me down. My father looks away as usual and Mila and James give me curious looks.

- So I wanted to ask you who this man was," my mother asks.

- I'm her husband," says Gabo, holding me close. I guess you're her mother.

- Yes, I am. I can't believe my daughter got married without telling us.

- I can't believe you're my mother, but you are," I replied, meeting her eyes.

- Alma, show her more respect. She's our mother after all," Mila said, getting up from her chair.

- She's your mother, not mine. She died for me the day my whole family turned their back on me because of you.

I get up and walk out of the dining room without waiting. This family has a lot of nerve. If it wasn't for Grandma who has always been there for me, I wouldn't be here. I feel tears rolling down my cheeks and I can't help it.

- It's okay, it's over. We can go back if that's what you want.

- No," I stammered against his chest. It's just that I'm so angry and hormones aren't helping. She's my mom, but even when it was tough, she didn't support me.

- You'll be fine. Easy," he whispers, kissing the top of my head. I'm here.

He puts one arm under my legs and the other behind my back before carrying me like a princess. I don't even have the strength to tell him to let me down when he takes us back to my room. The worst thing about this is that tomorrow is the party to announce my sister's wedding.

Chapter 22

Alma! We leave! Amber writes from the first floor.

- I'm coming, I say, rushing out of the room before being intercepted by Gabrielo.

- Stop running like that, please, he says and pulls me towards him. You might hurt yourself and slip.

- You always worry too much!

- That's what you said when you almost slipped down the stairs at home. If I were you, I'd stop right there.

- That was an accident. And it won't happen again.

- Alma! Amber shouted as she stared at me down the stairs.

- I have to go. Bye," I said, kissing Gabrielo, "I'll see you later.

- See you tonight," he said, taking me in his arms and coming close to my ear. I might be late. Whatever happens out there, stay strong. Call me if anything happens, I'll come as soon as I can.

I give him a smile before kissing him again. We part and I quickly go down to join my cousin. Amber glares at me before I wrap my arm around hers.

- Always late! I'm sure you'll be late for your own wedding ceremony.

- No doubt, but you'll be there to cover for me. You always are.

- If you believe that. Why isn't Gabrielo here?

- I could ask you the same question about Steven. The answer will always be the same: work.

- One day I'll flush his phone down the toilet. That way, no more interruptions, she exclaims, smiling in anticipation.

- It sounds strangely personal. Just turn it off without him noticing.

- Good idea! Let's head for the beauty salon. We have all the morning to be pampered like princesses!

So we spent all morning in a beauty salon reserved for the occasion. My husband really thinks of everything! That it is manicure, pedicure, hairstyle or make-up nothing was left behind. We even had a massage and a body treatment. I feel reborn. I had not taken the time to relax like that since our return from honeymoon.

- Tell me," Amber begins, "are you planning to wear heels with your dress?

- Just for the occasion. It will be 6 cm square heels so that I don't strain my back. I promised not to wear stiletto after all.

- Oh my. Pregnancy. If it wasn't for this child, you'd be even trendier. I still can't believe you actually gave up your signature stilettos.

- That's a good sign," I laughed. I have another five months of pregnancy to endure before I can have my baby in my arms. Hopefully, I'll still be able to run around on your birthday. If Gabrielo doesn't keep me at home.

- Life is so hard, Alma," laughed Amber. Meavy told me she was coming later. I knew I had forgotten to tell you something!

- Did you? She didn't tell me anything.

- She called me earlier because you didn't answer her. She'll meet us in the reception room.

The more the merrier. I go up to my room to put on my dress and shoes. I join Amber in the entrance and a driver comes to take us. I go up in the car which stops after twenty minutes of ride.

- Let's get this party started! A voice exclaims behind me, hugging me from behind.

- Meavy! It's nice to see you again," I said, giving her a hug.

- Me too! Amber, as sexy as ever, I see! I love it!

- The feeling is mutual, Amber replies, hugging her. And your teacher?

- I prefer being single, replies Meavy.

- So he dumped you, I concluded in unison with my cousin.

- Not at all! Meavy takes offense. I dumped him because I wasn't interested in him anymore.

- And why is that?

- I got tired of him. Are you happy? Enough of this chitchat! It's time to go show Chinchilla who we are.

I burst out laughing at my sister's nickname. Meavy never liked her and that's not going to change now. Even more after she hurt me so much. We enter the room and all eyes turn to us. I smile at people like nothing happened.

Almost half the people in this room know that I had a relationship with James. And their opinion on the subject is not... Very positive. Even more so because Mila was rumored to be pregnant when I hadn't been in five years of dating. That's part of the reason my parents urged me to stay away from him.

That way, Mila could secure her relationship with James's family, which, let's face it, was pretty well off. Except she wasn't pregnant.

- Alma, it's good to see you," my sister exclaims as she approaches my ex on her arm.

- I wasn't going to miss this for anything," I said, faking a smile as best I could. This is the wedding of the two people who have disappointed me the most in this world. How could I miss it? I even brought a date for the occasion.

Mila forces a smile and inhales before answering me.

- If you don't know how to keep a man around, there's nothing I can do about it," Mila sneers.

- And if you can't keep your zipper up," I say, turning to James and then Mila, "and you can't keep your thighs shut, I can't help that either. Just be careful you don't get an STD. After all, if you cheat once, why wouldn't you do it again?

- Be careful what you say," James threatens, glaring at me. Just because you're pregnant doesn't mean-

- That what? You can't lay a hand on me? I say with a chuckle. Try me. James tenses up without daring to approach me.

- Believe me, you're going to regret your words in a few minutes," I announced. Do you really want me to talk about what happened with Chris?

James blushes and backs away slightly. My sister turns to him and frowns. She raises her eyebrows to quietly question him.

- Don't act so surprised Mila.

- Stop the bullshit, you don't know anything, against James.

- Did you think you'd be the only one for him? I asked Mila. When he was already sleeping with Christian? It's like the saying goes, " Birds of a feather flock together. You've been acting out the story of your pregnancy. If you think I didn't know, you're wrong. Who knew you'd go as far as faking a miscarriage?

- I don't know what you're talking about," Mila snarled, still holding her head high.

- If you say so. We'll leave you to it. You have a lot to talk about, I guess.

The three of us head to the buffet and I help myself to some pastries. Meavy fills her plate and mine with whatever she can find without stopping.

- What happened with Christian? Amber asks, bringing a champagne flute to her mouth. I think I heard something but didn't understand everything.

- You'd better sit down," I say, leading her to a chair.

- What's up? she asks impatiently.

I glance at Meavy, who seems just as embarrassed as I am. Maybe we should have told her sooner.

- Christian, your brother, slept with my ex, James. Several times, no less.

Chapter 23

Amber chokes on her champagne and Meavy pats her back.

- I beg your pardon? It is a joke, right? My brother?

- I didn't want to tell you about it, but since I started I might as well finish.

Amber gets up and starts pacing. We see her brother at the back of the room and she excuses herself to go talk to him. I get up to follow her. Amber grabs Christian's arm before dragging him out of the room. We arrive on the balcony outside and I grab Amber's wrist.

- Amber, calm down, I asked.

- Calm down, she writhed. My brother slept with your ex!

She grabs Christian who lets her by the collar and throws him to the ground.

- Why, she blows with tears in her eyes. Why did you do that? Christian!

- Sorry, he says by raising his eyes.

Amber is about to slap him and I stop her. She turns to me and begins to calm down.

- What happened is done. He slept with him, so what? It's not like I can do anything about it. He asked me to forgive him and I've already accepted his apology," I say as I help Christian to his feet.

He thanks me and stands there. I caress his head and he finally meets my eyes. He is like my little brother. He made mistakes but he showed he was sorry. It's not like I forgave him right away. It took me a few months to get there but it's behind us.

- Go ahead," I said with a smile. I'm sure your boyfriend is waiting for you. I'll see you later. We all go back inside. Amber is still confused and angry about what happened. Nobody knows the whole story. Not to mention that we are all either good or evil, it just depends on who is telling the story.

Meavy takes a seat next to mine and turns to me.

- How did you know?

- I saw them. Chris apologized before I broke up with James. And he called me when we were at the club because he had done it again.

- Are you mad at him?

- Not really," I replied with a sigh. I feel like it's not really his fault. James took advantage of his emotional dependency knowing he wouldn't be able to deal with it. I feel rather sorry for him.

It took a lot of therapy for him to move on. Now that he's better, I'd rather put what happened behind us. He was tricked in some way.

- I don't understand how you can be so empathetic," Meavy sighed. I never know whether to admire you or be exasperated by your behavior.

- Admire me," I replied, "it will be better for my ego.

- Yes, ma'am. Don't you want me to rub your feet while you're at it?

- That's okay, I'd rather you convince my husband to let me work.

- No, thank you. This debate might end with me leaving in tears, completely traumatized and terrified.

- More seriously, when is he going to arrive? I've been bored since earlier.

- He should be here any minute. He loves you way too much to leave you here. You guys are like tic and tac. Always stuffed together.

- Leave me alone," I mumbled. Amber, make peace with your brother. He's already admitted his mistakes so it's okay, right?

- I'll try, she says. I can't believe he did that, she hisses. With James of all people.

- No one had noticed, I said quietly. He had started acting weird. He was always fidgety and nervous. When he told me everything, it got worse so I had to drag him to see a therapist. Now that he's better, let's stop making him feel guilty.

- Why didn't you say anything? Amber asks.

- When I realized, it had already been a while. Christian was so dependent on James that I thought if it all stopped at once, he'd do something regrettable. That's why I didn't say anything.

There is a silence around us and no one dares to speak. I lean against my seat and watch the chandelier above our heads glow.

- Alma, your parents are coming towards us.

All but them. Please. I don't have the strength to fight them now.

- Alma, what did you say to your sister again? My mother asks.

- Mom, how nice to see you! I'm very well, thank you. How are you?

- Let's skip the formalities. What did you say to her to get her in such a state? My mother insists, grabbing my arm.

- Nothing at all. She left on her own to talk with James. What does that have to do with me?

- Stop lying to me, Alma," my father intervenes with a stern look. This is not the time to cause a scene in public.

- So what? She's crying because she wants to. I didn't force her to cry or make a scene. It's not my fault she's so ill-behaved.

- I don't allow you," my mother grumbles. You'd better keep your arrogance to yourself.

She tightens her grip on me as I try to pull away. One hand grabs my mother's and violently throws her off. My husband takes me in his arms and pulls me away from her.

- I'm going to have to ask you to stop making rough contact with my wife. As you have noticed, she is pregnant," Gabrielo says with a threatening look.

- You think you're going to teach me how to handle my daughter? My mother takes offense.

- I believe that I am also going to teach you to respect her if you continue, Gabrielo counters by squeezing me against him.

- Excuse me?! If she is in wrong, she deserves to be told. She needs to learn from her mistakes.

- A man who marries his mistress leaves her seat vacant. She just reminded Mila of that. What is it that is shocking to you? My husband asks with a sneer.

- I won't allow you to talk to me like that," exclaims my mother, approaching us.

- I don't need anyone's permission," my husband replies without blinking. If you have any problems, go and complain somewhere else. There's no one here to put up with your whining.He takes me by the hand and leads me to sit down. I sit on his lap and watch the big screen in the center of the room.

- I have prepared a little surprise to brighten up the party.

- What did you prepare?

- A little personalized gift. Nothing too fancy. Don't worry about it.

He puts a kiss on my temple and wraps his arms around me. I lay my head in the hollow of his neck and he holds me close. Noise comes from the center of the room. I turn my gaze and watch the screen that has just turned on.

- Enjoy the show, Stellina.

I frown, trying to understand. What is he up to? An image appears with James and Mila both smiling in each other's arms. Then the image evaporates to make way for a video. My sister drunkenly kissing a man in a nightclub.

A series of images of her heading to a hotel with him and entering a room follow. All eyes turn to my sister who doesn't know where to stand. She steps back and a new image appears. This time with James. He appears in a bar playing footsie with a woman near him.

He goes into the bathroom with her and comes out a few minutes later. We see him continue to party and head into a brothel. The rest of the scene takes place inside. He is surrounded by women and men who are busy doing.... Their business. The screen goes blank and we hear a huge noise resounding.

Mila has just slapped James. She seems to have tears in her eyes and leaves the reception room. James leaves in a very relaxed way after her. Quite a show.

- If they intended to get married, it was necessary to start by being faithful. Don't you think, Meavy asks as she joins us.

- That's true, but it's none of our business. Let's just be present.

- I agree with you on this one. Amber just left with Christian. They seem to have decided to make peace. Even though Amber looked like she was about to punch him in the face.

- That's good. Amber remains who she is. Her impulsiveness has not changed, I say by repressing a yawn.

- For the moment, you are going to go to sleep and to rest, Gabrielo intervenes by looking at me.

- Let's go, I am exhausted.

We enter the car and I finally relax. This day was exhausting. In all the meanings of the word. The driver starts and I let myself go against my husband.

- Hard day?

- Between the beauty salon and the guests, you have no idea. Your gift was sensational. Where did you get that information?

- I have a long arm, he just answers.

- I do not doubt it. I just got the proof. It was incredible, especially the look on Mila's face. I think we'll be able to get back early.

- We could have a vacation here," Gabrielo suggested, his eyes shining.

- Why do I get the feeling that you take every opportunity not to work?

- Because I do. I'd much rather spend an hour with you than an hour at work.

- Thanks, but you'll have to work if you want us to have a roof over our heads. Since I'm not working now.

- I know," Gabrielo grumbles.

- You can't keep giving your assistant a hard time. He'll die of overexertion at this rate.

- He'll take a vacation when we get back," he says, putting his head on my shoulder.

- Before I forget," I said, stroking his hair. Cole offered to decorate the baby's room for me since we didn't think of that. What do you think?

- Do we have to say yes? He asks while grimacing.

- Gabrielo.

- It's okay, tell him to settle for the minimum.

- What a minimum. Meavy will join him in a few days so he can get started. Don't forget to call him and tell him.

- Why me and not you?

- Because he's your best friend. He'll be happy to hear you tell him.

Gabrielo sighs before taking me in his arms. We arrive finally in front of the house where noises of broken glasses are heard since the outside. Shouts come from the kitchen if I am not mistaken.

What the hell ?

Chapter 24

We come up and Yuma is standing in front of the half-open kitchen door. He's watching the scene inside while eating popcorn like he is at the movies.

- What's up? Gabrielo asks as he comes closer.

- Mila and James," my brother replies, swallowing a handful of popcorn. They've been like this since they arrived. I hope they don't break all the dishes there are. Otherwise, I'll have to figure out how to find another dish to eat off of.

- You and the food, I sighed.

- Leave me alone. Besides, as long as I don't get fat, that is the main thing.

- If you say so. What are they fighting about?

- Because of what happened at the party. Ignore them," he says, wrapping his arm around my neck. Right now, I have something to tell you.

He takes me into the living room where Gabrielo follows us. We sit on a couch in the middle of the room.

- Christian... .

- Slept with James. Yes, I know. I don't necessarily blame him because I know the circumstances under which it happened.

- What circumstances? Yuma asks with a frown.

I lean against Gabrielo, feeling a pang of exhaustion. He takes me in his arms and I continue my story. Yuma decided to wait for my explanation before going to see our cousin and I am grateful to him. He already didn't go to assault him without knowing the truth.

- "We were all at a party that night. It was Meavy's brother who organized it. I think you remember it," I said, seeing that he was widening his eyes. There was a lot of booze, and they gave out ecstasy and other drugs to the guests. Enough to last the whole night.

We were all there, Meavy, Amber, Christian, Mila, James, you and me. The party was in full swing and everyone had scattered. I stayed with Meavy and we were playing the bottle game and truth or dare. I drank so many shots of vodka that I started to feel sick.

Meavy walked me upstairs to sit for a few minutes. I wanted to walk around the floor and started opening random rooms. At the end of the hallway, I opened the door slowly and met Christian's eyes, in bed with James. They were having sex.

I walked out quietly before heading back downstairs to the living room. Meavy found me and I told her everything. Christian came in shortly after and pulled me aside so he could talk to me. I still remember what he said to me.

- I'm sorry! he exclaimed, fiddling with his hair. I know what I did was wrong. I shouldn't have slept with James. It's just that...

Tears were streaming down his panic-stricken face. He was starting to pull his hair and I could see handfuls of it falling to the floor. A sob shook him before he fell to the ground, his head in his hands.

- I'm sorry, I'm sorry, I'm sorry," he chanted, sobbing. I can't stop this. I'm sorry. I just can't do it. I can't help it. I need him.

- I noticed," I said, leaning against a door. I saw the way you looked at him, but I thought I was wrong. Could you just leave me alone for a few moments?

- Alma, please.

- No, not this time. Do you realize that you think you need him?

Christian lowered his head in shame.

- Go away. "

- That's how I knew what was going on between those two, I concluded.

- And you've stayed with James all this time? Yuma asked as he stood up.

- Not really. This all happened a week before I left. I was going to end it with him and his affair with Mila made it easier.

- Alma, I. . . . I don't know what to say.

- Then don't say anything. As of today I have a stable, well-paying job, I'm married and I'm having a child. I don't blame him because he opened my eyes to what kind of person James was. I just wish I had known before I wasted so much time on him.

I am seriously starting to feel the fatigue coming on. This day has already been full of twists and turns. Gabrielo speaks, but I can't concentrate on what he is saying. My eyes keep closing until I can't stay awake anymore.

When Gabrielo said that my mother had gathered my entire family, he wasn't kidding. There are even people I haven't seen since my junior high days. Not to mention the heavy atmosphere in the room. It almost feels like someone has died.

- The reason we are all here today is to talk about the events that took place yesterday. Photoshopped images were shown at Mila and James' engagement party," my mom continues, turning to me. Don't you have anything to say?

- Like what? I saw the video like everyone else, if that's what you want to know.

- You should apologize to your sister. Making such a montage for revenge is not right.

- What's next? Don't you want me to kneel down too? If I had so much free time, I would spend it doing something else. If you didn't want people to be suspicious, you should have raised her differently. Who steals their sister's fiancé to begin with?

Whispers cross the room and eyes turn to my mother.

- I will not allow you to talk to me like this! she shouts, getting up.

- I do allow myself," I object. "I will apologize on one condition.

- What is that? Asks my mother more calmly.

- Where is the baby?

My mother's gaze flickers silently. Mila glances at James without daring to speak. The room has fallen silent again as we wait for my mother's answer.

- What are you talking about?

- When I broke off my engagement, you told me that Mila was pregnant. And then that she had a miscarriage. Except no one has heard anything about this pregnancy, let alone this miscarriage. So I would like an explanation. Why did you lie to me?

Chapter 25

Why? Because your sister was a better choice for James. Who would want to help someone else's child instead of their own?

- I beg your pardon? I exclaimed, my eyes widening. Someone else's child? I'm as much your daughter as Mila is.

- Stop lying to yourself," she replied, approaching me. You will always be Isla Pearson's daughter. Not mine! Let me get this straight. We're not related.

So that's what it was all about.

- Carmela! My father shouted, reacting for the first time since I arrived.

- Did you think I was going to keep my mouth shut? Carmela continues. If you hadn't had that fling with a whore, we wouldn't be in this mess! She had to die and her children ended up with us!

- Carmela, shut up!

- On top of that, she ended up losing some of her memories in an accident. Do you know how I feel since that day she called me mom?!

Memories start to come back instantly. My mother's face, her smiles, her voice. All my memories that were confused after the accident that happened a few years ago are coming back in order. How things actually happened and especially Carmela and Mila.

- A whore? I repeated, raising my voice. Carmela, if you hadn't had an affair with a married man, we simply wouldn't be here. I have to thank you though, otherwise I wouldn't have met my husband today.

The murmurs start again in the room, accompanied this time by giggles. Gabrielo squeezes my hand, pulls me towards him and starts caressing my shoulder affectionately. I hold on to him, caressing my belly. It seems that strong emotions really don't do me any good lately.

Carmela stares at me completely speechless. Mila joins her before she starts to defend her mother.

- Shut up," I ordered, glaring at her. If your mother hadn't lured my father into a bar 20 years ago, you wouldn't be here. If she had any respect for another woman's marriage, if she cared about anything other than money, you wouldn't be in this house and my mother wouldn't be six feet under right now. So, I'm going to repeat myself Mila Rodriguez: shut up.

- I won't tolerate this! Her mother says.

- Don't forget that according to the terms of the will, if I'm married before I'm thirty, 50% of the shares of the family business that belonged to my mother go to me. And I don't intend to give it up.

I detach myself from Gabrielo to get up and leave the room without adding anything. That's why I hadn't missed the family reunions.

Remembering so many things exhausted me. Not to mention the fights that are always going on with Carmela. I sit on the floor, breathing in deeply when a sharp pain hits my stomach.

- What's wrong? Gabrielo panics as he gets down to my level.

- My stomach hurts. It's nothing. It will pass," I answered, breathing heavily. It's probably just contractions.

Gabrielo took me in his arms before getting up and heading outside.

- Where are we going?

- To the hospital," Gabrielo replies, putting me in the passenger seat.

- I'm telling you that -Ouch!

- That's what I thought too.

Final verdict: the doctor's opinion is rarely in your favor.

I'm on bed rest for the next three days. My grandmother forbade anyone to come bother me. The doctor announced that it was stress and accumulated fatigue that had put me in this state. Gabrielo, who took it very seriously, wanted to take me back to New York, but I refused. That's how I ended up stuck on this bed for the last two days.

-You really don't want to go home? My husband tries again.

- Gabrielo, you know I love you, but you're starting to piss me off. We've had this conversation before and my answer won't change. Besides, traveling always stresses me out.

- We'll leave as soon as this whole wedding thing is over. You got it?

- All right. By the time we get back, I want you to have called Cole and Meavy to fix up the baby's room. And I want to be able to work from home without having to listen to you complain.

- Why would you want to work?

- Bridal fashion week is in a few months. I need to work on some new designs. And fast.

- Whatever you need. It's not like I'm here to force you to do anything. Just take it easy on yourself.

- I promise. Now come lie down with me. I crave your company after you left me for your work.

- Your wish is my command," he concedes as he comes to kiss me.

Today I am finally free to move from the bed after three days of forced rest. Meavy came to visit me as usual before she had to go back to the United States. If I understood correctly, she received an important job from a big client. She's going to take care of the baby's room until we get back with Cole.

- Ready ? Gabrielo asks as he gets out of the shower.

- No, and I probably never will be. Why do we have to watch this farce?

- Because Mrs. Moretti said she was well enough to attend yesterday when she met her family. And since I'm a good husband and I love you, I'm going along for moral support.

- I should have kept my mouth shut," I mumbled as I got out of bed.

- Unfortunately for us, it's too late to turn back. Up and at 'em, let's go for the tasting.

- I'm outraged, frankly. I didn't even get a cake for my wedding and I'm going to be involved in hers. I hope she chokes on her cake.

Gabrielo laughs before taking me in his arms and kissing my forehead.

- You'll have your cake, your dress and your perfect wedding," he says. Anything you want as long as you stay with me.

I let myself go temporarily and he takes the opportunity to pass his hand on my belly. A smile appears on his face and he holds me close to him.

- I want a girl, he announces while looking at me.

- I hope she'll make you wear frilly dresses and drink tea. Now let's go.

We leave my room hand in hand under the glance of my family. Amber waves to me and walks with Steven to his car. I do the same before deciding to turn around. The car goes into the street in the direction of the bakery.

- I want to go home, I complain.

- If we're here, it's all your fault," Gabrielo retorts without taking his eyes off the landscape. You're going to do me a favor and stop complaining. Smile, you're going to eat some cake.

- Youhou! I've never been so happy in my life," I said ironically. Honestly, eating cake with my half-sister and my ex couldn't have been better!

- Breathe, Alma, breathe. Everything is going to be okay. We're going to sit down with the others and go back.

- You know very well that's not true. Even optimism doesn't work that well anymore.

We get out of the car before going into the bakery. Everyone else seems to have arrived before us. We go towards Amber and Steven at first.

- What's the matter?

- The cake is still not ready and your mother - sorry, Carmela is making a scene in the kitchen.

- Great, as if the day wasn't already long enough, I sighed.

I sat down on a chair next to my cousin, resting my head on her shoulder. Gabrielo and Steven have gone to get us drinks while we wait for the cake. I'm starting to fall asleep when I hear a throat clearing.

James is standing in front of us, watching me without saying anything.

- What?

- I'd like to talk to you," he asks as we move forward. Alone, if possible.

Chapter 26

What's the deal? I have nothing to say to you," I replied, my eyes glued to my phone screen.

- Alma, please," James begged.

- No. When I wanted an explanation for your cheating, remember what you just said? "Why should I explain anything to you?"

- I just want us to have a proper conversation between adults.

- I don't have anything to say to you and I don't want to know anything more about you. If you have something to tell me, talk to my husband. Get lost!

James turns back without replying. I see Gabo arriving in our direction with a pastry for me, my favorite one at that. I smile at him before kissing him and thanking him. He sits me on his lap while waiting for the time of the tasting to come. The cake designer arrives soon and we start to test the cakes.

- What's the matter? Gabrielo asks as I sway over him.

- I want to go to the bathroom," I whispered in response.

- Go then. I'll wait here with your cake.

- Thank you," I said.

I get up quickly before heading down a hallway where the bathroom is located. This is already the second time since we arrived. This child is really starting to weigh heavily on my bladder. I hurry to finish my business and go out again. I come face to face with James who seems to be waiting for me since earlier.

- What do you want now?

- To talk to you. I only want you to listen to me.

- Speak then, I answer curtly.

He looks at his feet while fiddling with his fingers.

- You were right to leave me," he said, looking into my eyes. I'm sorry for the pain I caused you.

- What do you want? I asked, squinting my eyes. Even if you had regrets, you should have expressed them earlier. If you're telling me this now, it means you want something.

- I wanted to ask you a favor. Leave Mila alone, please. She doesn't deserve to be dragged into our mess.

- She does and you know it as well as I do. If she hadn't been sleeping with you behind my back, we wouldn't be in this mess.

- Alma-

- I told you to stop saying my name with that dirty mouth of yours. You know what the worst part of this story is? I asked with a bitter smile. It was at my house that you were meeting. You didn't even have an ounce of respect for me so why should I have any for you now?

- Alma, listen to me," he said, stepping forward and grabbing my arm. Leave Mila alone. I'm not joking with you.

- I'm not joking with you either. I told you that, didn't I? "Fool me and I'll make you bite your fingers off so hard you'll wish you'd never crossed my path." This is just the beginning. What would your beloved mom say if she found out about Alexia and Mathéo? Not to mention the way you used to play with Christian.

- When did you...?

- Since the beginning, before we even started dating. Nothing can be hidden from me, you see. When I want to know something, I use every means at my disposal. Did you really think I was going to keep your secret after what you did?

- It's none of your business," he hisses.

- Alexia is one of my closest friends. I kept the secret in the past to stay with you. It's all over now. Alexia has been having some problems lately. I'll make sure they're taken care of before I leave.

I break away from his grasp before heading to the room and back to my husband. Everything will be known in due time. Nothing and no one will stop me from seeking justice.

- Alma! I haven't been able to talk to you since you got here. How have you been? James' mother asks.

- I'm doing fine. How about you?

- I'm doing great. Congratulations on your wedding and your pregnancy by the way. It's a little late, but don't hold it against me. So tell me, how is life in New York?

- Wonderful," I replied, smiling at her. How is your husband doing?

- Very well, thank you. I'm sorry for what James did to you. I know you don't need my apology, but I am sorry. I feel like I've failed as a mother, she sighs. What a failure.

James enters the room with Mila by his side. He sees me out of the corner of his eye with his mother. I smile briefly before resuming my conversation. He walks over to us and grabs my arm.

- Can you let go of me, please?

- How about we go talk? He suggests with a clenched jaw.

- No, thank you. Let me go.

- Leave her alone, his mother orders, trying to separate me from his grip.

He's really starting to hurt me.

- Take your hand away, says Gabrielo, coming up behind him. Quickly. Make the most of the fact that I'm still willing to talk.

Gabrielo grabs James' hand and forces him to let go of me gently. I see my ex's face twist in pain as Gabrielo looks furious. He makes the mother and son leave so we can talk quietly.

- What's going on here?

- Nothing, I just told my brother-in-law that I have become aware of all the things he has buried in the past. He was ashamed and I swore to reveal everything. He didn't like it, that's it.

- Alma," Gabrielo sighs, pulling me closer to him. I don't care what you do because I trust you.

- I know you do.

- But don't act like you're not pregnant. You are going to drive me crazy. Just knowing that your ex is around all the time even when

I'm not around is already getting on my nerves so stop acting like nothing's changed.

- Gabrielo," I said, taking him in my arms. That's so sweet. I appreciate you being jealous and worried. I'll be careful so stop getting stressed out.

- I hope so. Otherwise, I'll handcuff you to the bed until we get back," he says, kissing my forehead.

I laugh at his words before standing up. I still hope it doesn't come to that. That would mean a lot of fun in a certain way. Everyone seems to be busy tasting cake and talking. We go outside to get some fresh air.

- Alma! says a voice behind me.

Who is calling me again?

- Christian! I exclaimed as I spotted my cousin. I missed you!

- I missed you too," he said, taking him in my arms.

Gabrielo grabs me by the waist, preventing me from approaching him. I turn to him by frowning.

- What is wrong? I asked.

- Who is it? my husband asks as he watches Christian draw near.

- It is Amber's brother, Christian.

- The famous one, he murmured.

- Yes, now let me greet him, I whispered.

We continue to look at each other before he releases me. I take Christian in my arms and we return to join the others. Amber joined us accompanied by Steven and Yuma. The tasting ends and we return each one on our side. The trip in the car happens in a good mood.

- Gabrielo ?

- Hum ?

- We could make a detour before going back ?

- No problem. Where are we going?

- Follow my lead.

I lead Gabrielo to the location. He parks and we get out of the car in the center of town.

- Do you want to tell me where we are going now?

- To the cemetery and then to the notary.

Chapter 27

Who died? Gabrielo asks nervously.

- One of my best friends. I knew her before Meavy and we hung out for a while. She got married early, then had a daughter. Not long after that, she got it into her head to tour the world with her family to make memories for her daughter before she had to go to elementary school.

Gabrielo shook my hand and I continued my story.

- I heard from her regularly and we stayed in touch. I have not heard from her or her husband since last month. All my attempts have come to nothing. Until the day of the "family reunion". The notary called me to tell me that they died in a ship accident.

- That's why you've been so depressed lately.

- Maybe I was. It must have been the news that was too much. We're here now. It's a good thing we changed all our clothes to black. Let's go.

The funeral ended quickly between the crying and the people collapsing in grief. Some children were there without realizing why. I shed a few silent tears that Gabrielo wiped away without saying a word. After giving our condolences, we went straight to the notary. The day was already long enough, no need to drag it out.

- Welcome, please come in," the notary asked as he welcomed us into his office. Sit down, I'm sorry to have made you come from so far away. I had no other choice.

- And the others? I asked, looking around the empty room.

- They will be here any moment.

As announced, two women and a man entered the room ten minutes later. A little girl entered after them and joined us.

- Very well. We'll be able to start," said the notary, taking out three letters. Mr. Liam Smith has decided to leave all of his antique cars to Mr. Andrew Smith as well as his two vacation homes in France. Mrs. Elisabeth Smith bequeaths all her jewelry to her sister Lindsay McParlay. Mr. Frank McParlay will receive 10 million dollars to help found his company.

He closes both letters before opening the last one.

- Miss Cordelia Smith will receive all the stock her parents owned in the Smith Co. corporation when she comes of age. Until then, they will go to her guardian Mrs. Alma Moretti along with the rest of the property they owned.

- I beg your pardon? I exclaimed, suddenly understanding the notary's words.

He glanced at me and continued reading the will.

- Mrs. Alma Moretti becomes the legal guardian of Cordelia Smith unless she refuses to take on this responsibility, in which case she will be placed in the family of a close volunteer," the notary continued without paying me any attention.

What the hell is this? I didn't even know about this story. I glance at Gabo, who looks impassive. He must be digesting the information in his own way.

- Cordelia Smith will therefore receive all the remaining assets of her parents when she comes of age, such as the family home, the sixteen vacation homes abroad, their fortune of over 55 billion dollars and their stock market shares. Ten million dollars will be distributed to charities and orphanages. For the time being, the management of all his assets is in the hands of Alma Moretti and her spouse.

- What do you mean? Lindsay exclaims as she stands up. My niece's custody should be rightfully ours! We are her family. Alma Moretti remains a mere stranger.

- Calm down, the notary orders. The will of the deceased must be respected no matter what. They have left a letter for this kind of problem, he says, taking out a fourth letter. Your attention, please.

"The custody of our daughter must go to Alma, she is the person we trust the most. Lindsay would end up squandering all that hard-earned money without realizing it. As for Andrew... He likes to hang out too much at night to give himself time to take care of a child. He definitely remembers the last time he babysat. Frank for his part has already stated that he does not want a child and his lifestyle is too unstable to entrust our daughter to him.

That's why we are entrusting you with the custody of our beloved daughter, Alma.

Take good care of her. We are counting on you.

Elizabeth and Liam."

I sigh before standing up.

- That will be all, won't it?

- I just need a few signatures for the official papers and to explain your role going forward. I'll have to ask the others to leave the room.

The notary begins his explanations, pausing a few times to have papers signed. Little Cordelia has not moved an ear since she arrived in the office. As if something had broken in her. We finish this interview and I turn to Cordelia.

- Lia?" I called, holding out my hand.

She raises her head to meet my eyes. I bend down to her height to caress her head.

- It's been a long time since we've seen each other, right? Shall we go?

She nods weakly.

I take her in my arms before going outside. Once outside, Gabrielo takes her from my arms and continues walking towards the car.

- Gabrielo," I say, moving closer to him. I can carry her.

- No way. You're already four and a half months pregnant, it's not even a consideration.

- But Lia...

- She's doing great, look. She even fell asleep. We'll talk in the car.

It just so happens that the car was ten meters away from us.

- You don't want to keep her, do you? I asked once I was settled in my seat.

- I especially want to know how to do it now. We're having a baby. We decided to adopt Max and now we have a little girl. We're supposed to be back in New York in three weeks and this child needs to go to school, not to mention all the other arrangements we have to make.

- So we're keeping her?

- She stays with us. She's not an object and I'm sure that if her parents asked you to take care of her, it's for a good reason. Let us respect their last will.

I kiss Gabrielo on the cheek and he catches me before kissing me on the lips.

- Yuck! A voice exclaims from the back of the car.

- I thought you were asleep," I say, glancing at Cordelia.

- I'm hungry," she said in a small voice.

- Then let's stop and eat something. It's already 7 p.m. and I haven't eaten anything since 12. What do you want to eat?

- Pizza. And ice cream too. Please.

- Let's go for ice cream and pizza.

Gabrielo starts the car. During the whole drive, Cordelia seemed to be doing better. All she did was talk to Gabrielo to distract herself while I tried to sleep.

- Alma?

- Yes, corazón. What's up?

- Do you have a baby in your belly? Lia asks, pointing to her belly.

- Yes, I do.

- How do you make babies?

I freeze at this question. Usually, adults try to come up with a believable story to give to children. I have no idea what to say to that. The story about the storks? Santa Claus? My brain is trying to come up with a believable answer and can't.

- Do you really want to know? Gabrielo asks, glancing at her through the rearview mirror.

- Yes!" replies Lia, shaking her head vigorously.

- You need a boy and a girl. And they should be naked, begins Gabrielo.

- Why naked?

- For nothing! I say while raising the voice before pinching Gabrielo with the hand.

- Ouch! What? He takes offense.

- Shut up. That's not something to say to a three-year-old.

- But remember, she asked for it.

- Gabrielo, stop talking nonsense to her," I whispered in her ear.

- I only tell the truth," he said.

- If you continue with your truths, you will see. Her parents trust us and no three-year-old needs to know that kind of thing!

- It is good, he abdicated while throwing a glance to Cordelia. You'll know when you're old enough.

- A wise decision. Before I forget, the ultrasound to find out the sex of the baby is in three days. The obstetrician arrives the day after tomorrow.

Chapter 28

[Cordelia in media]

- Are you sulking? Gabrielo asks, wrapping his arms around me.

I give him a sideways glance before going back to playing with Lia. What a jerk! How dare he say that to me when it' s his fault I'm like this now!

- I'm sorry. I swear to you I'm sorry. I said it without thinking.

- If you said it, it's because you thought it," I replied as we went up to our room.

- Alma, listen to me.

- No, you listen to me. Since I'm so fat, you can sleep in the guest room where there's more room and I can sleep with Cordelia. Good night.

I'm slamming the door in his face.

- We sleep? Lia asks, tilting her head to one side.

- We'll wash up first. Then we'll go to sleep.

- And the mister?

- Leave him alone, he's a big boy. He can look after himself. Shall we go?

The next morning, Cordelia woke me up at seven to go and play. I'm willing to take her parents' place, but we're going to have to set up some rules. I'm heavily pregnant, I need my sleep and the baby is getting heavier and heavier. My sleep is pri-mor-dial.

- Honey, I need to get some more sleep, please," I pleaded, looking at the child in front of me.

- But it's already sunny," she said, making puppy eyes. It's time to get up.

I sighed as I sat down on the bed.

- It's time to get up," I breathed, carrying her in my arms. What do you want to eat?

- Brioche and hot chocolate!

- Is that all?

Lia nods and smiles. I walk into the kitchen and see Gabrielo reading the paper. I had forgotten that he was an early riser. He looks up and smiles when he sees us. He stands up and takes Cordelia from my arms.

- What's the matter? I asked as I let him do it.

Cordelia gives him a confused look and opens her arms to return with me.

- Cordelia," Gabrielo calls softly. You'll crush the baby if you don't stop being carried by Alma. You don't want that to happen, do you?

- No," Lia replies, shaking her head.

- I'll carry you if you want, but no more carrying for Alma. Come on.

Cordelia wraps her arms around Gabrielo's neck. I go to the cupboards to get out some food. A mocaccino for my husband and a hot chocolate and brioche for my new daughter. I serve them everything and start drinking my juice with my pain au chocolat.

- Ahhh," Lia says, handing Gabrielo a piece of brioche.

He opens his mouth without thinking and she stuffs a piece of brioche inside. Lia giggles and fidgets in her chair. I smile when I see them both. They look like father and daughter.

- Alma?

- Hm?

- Are you still mad at me?

- Yes. You still called me fat when I'm over four months pregnant.

- I swear I was joking. And technically I just said you got fatter than I thought.

Silence.

- Can I come back and sleep with you?

I glance at Lia who nods.

- My mummy used to say that you shouldn't go to sleep when you're angry," she says. If you do, you'll regret it later.

I nod and get up to clear away, but Gabo beats me to it. He finishes tidying up and sits down next to me, putting a hand on my stomach. He strokes it and I feel a jolt.

- It moved," Gabrielo exclaims with a huge smile on his face.

- It's the first time I've felt it," I smiled, putting my hand on his. It seems that the baby prefers his father.

- Me too," Cordelia exclaims and holds out her little hand. Gabrielo puts her on his lap so that she can touch my belly.

She flinches when she feels the blow before turning back to me with bright eyes.

- When are we going to see the baby? Tomorrow? she asks, holding my hand.

- A long time from now, Lia. Today we're going to the doctor to see the baby. Do you want to come?

- Yes!

- Then we are going to get you all dressed up.

We go upstairs to get ready. I finish dressing Cordelia and give her a kiss on the cheek. She starts to laugh out loud while holding her cheeks. This child is simply adorable. How can I resist her adorable face?

- Let's go, little princess," says Gabrielo, putting her on his shoulders.

I follow them out of the house and get into the car. We go straight to the obstetrician. She lays me on the bed and starts applying the cold gel to my belly.

- Let's see. Do you want to know the gender of the child?

I glance at Gabrielo who answers for me.

- We'd rather have the surprise when the baby is born.

- That's fine. The baby is very healthy. It moves well and is growing well. That's all for now. Keep it up and you'll be fine.

- Thank you very much, doctor.

I wipe my stomach and sit up.

- I have a question," Gabrielo intervenes, approaching the doctor to whisper in his ear.

- Of course you can," the doctor replies, laughing.

- I knew it! he exclaims with a smile. You can do sports.

- Ah yes. . Great," I say in defeat. Goodbye doctor!

We leave the office and Gabo is still as happy as ever.

- Cordelia, do you want to go to the zoo? I asked as I fastened her belt.

- To see the animals?

- Of course. How about it?

- I wanna go to the zoo. Can we have cotton candy?

- As you wish. Let's go, Mister Sportsman.

- You're going to do it too.

- With that belly. Even if you paid me millions, I wouldn't move.

- Alma, it's good for your health," Gabrielo countered.

- Of course it is. I'm on maternity leave. I intend to make the most of it. Just so we're clear, I'm not going to do any sports.

We had an amazing day. We really did.

Even Cordelia fell asleep on the way over and we let her sleep alone in an adjacent room. And then Mila and Carmen stormed into our room just as I was about to sleep. How convenient.

- Can't it wait until tomorrow? I asked, on the verge of a nervous breakdown.

- No!" Mila cried, walking towards us.

I put my head on Gabrielo's shoulder, hoping to fall asleep despite the noise in the house.

- What's going on? Gabo asks, glaring at Mila.

- I-I. .

- Just talk. If you have nothing to say, you know where the door is.

- Alexia. She came with a child. She said he was James'.

- Finally," I said, yawning.

- What do you mean 'finally'? Mila asks as she approaches me.

- That story happened three years ago. I knew about it, but I never said anything. Keeping this child was up to her and nobody else. She just came to claim what he owed her for years.

- Alma, you don't understand. My marriage is really going to fall apart this time. He'll have to marry her.

- So what? I replied. I have nothing to do with that. It's none of my business.

- Alma. Help me, please," begged Mila.

- You want help? Give her a spare room while you wait. I'll take care of the rest in the morning.

Mila and Carmen finally leave our room, which Gabo gets up and locks.

- What's on your mind now? he asks, kissing me.

- For the moment: nothing. - Did you call this girl here ?

- To be honest, I didn't even know where she was. I will think about it, the night is long.

- And a night of love only lasts a moment, so let me enjoy it.

Chapter 29

I am standing in front of Mila. Everyone in the house has gone out to do something. She sits down on the dining table and stares at me without saying anything.

- Why? I ask as I put down my cup of tea.

- Why?

- Why did you sleep with James behind my back?

- You want to know the truth," she laughed. I was dating James before he got involved with you. He went out with you thinking you could help him with some financial problems. His business was going bankrupt and he needed money.

- He could have asked his parents," I said, staring at her.

- What for? His mother was clear as he didn't want to take over the family business. He had to prove himself without relying on his family.

- And you're going to tell me that you accepted this compromise," I said. You're far too proud for that.

- You think I had a choice? He had borrowed money from loan sharks and he had to pay it back as soon as possible. He had a choice: plata o plomo. They had made it clear that if anyone was ever involved in this, everything would have gone to hell.

Mila sighs and brushes her hair back before looking at me.

- You all think life is great, but none of you know what he's been through. He slept with Christian, so what? I knew about it, the only rule between us was that everything had to be private.

- Doesn't the fact that he's cheating on you bother you? I asked intrigued.

The proud Mila knew when to get off her high horse. She clenched her jaw and took a sip of coffee.

- I'd rather he did it openly and for me to know than behind my back. It's his life and his body, he's free to do what he wants. If he really wanted to cheat on me, he would have done it anyway.

- What a way to think.

- I get that from my mother," she smiled. Why did you forgive Christian but not me?

- Because Christian isn't my sister. I trusted you. I really did. I was sure you would never betray my trust. Except I didn't expect anything from Christian.

- You all think I'm the bad guy in this story, except I was actually James' girlfriend. He fell in love with you by spending time with you. I ended up alone, and people kept comparing us even in public.

Mila's point of view

The comments in public, the criticism from my father, the criticism from my mother for not doing as well as my half-sister. All because she was going to get engaged at the last minute.

Everyone thinks my mother must have been happy. Well, she wasn't. She called me a homewrecker. She'd done the same thing I'd done to get us off the streets. To get away from gang wars and prostitution.

After some time with James, I knew that the only thing that would keep him around was a child. He was finally starting to come around.

I had a nervous pregnancy and my mother hid it by making my recovery look like a miscarriage.Alma puts her empty cup in front of me and glares at me.

- Is that why you decided to invite me to the engagement party? she asks curtly. Did you want to show me that you were better than me? Why did you use me instead of just asking me for help?

No. It's not that. Things are much more complicated than they seem. James isn't just a sex-crazed jerk. I'm not just a gold digger. The problem is, you'll never be able to put yourself in our shoes.

Not you, the little princess. Daddy loved you so much that he was always nagging me to be more like you.

His perfect daughter.

And after you left without saying anything, he decided to erase you from his life. You didn't have the courage to seek an explanation or to leave properly. You just ran away. You left us behind as if we didn't matter. Whether it's your father, your twin or your grandmother.

You ran away without a trace. Like a coward.

I can understand how I hurt you and betrayed you with James. Except the others didn't deserve that. They didn't deserve the sleepless nights they spent worrying or the tears they shed after thinking they'd lost you forever.

- We got into this because you were the only way we could get that much money in that short amount of time. James paid you back, didn't he?

Alma nods, looking stern.

- I came to you for help, but my mother was putting you through hell and you were doing everything to avoid me. I was lucky if I saw you, even if only on the street at the time.- It was the worst possible solution," said Alma.

- They often say the end justifies the means," I sighed. It's probably not right, but I couldn't let James risk his life. Not after what he had done for me.

If his business was going bankrupt, it was my fault after all. He was extorted a fortune to keep pictures taken without our knowledge off social media.

Pictures of me, my mother and Alma at the time. My mother was already having a hard time with this new family life that had been pushed on her. I knew she wouldn't be able to get over it. Alma...

I had noticed that she was not well. She had developed a complex because my mother thought that taking it out on her would make her feel better. Except she just needed help, not a way out.

James paid up without thinking twice. And since then, we've stuck together.

Except that after thinking about it all night, I decided to give up. We've reached a point where we don't know why we're together anymore. I'm grateful for everything James has done for me, but

I want to start over, away from my mother and all these problems.

I stand up before getting down on my knees and bowing my head.

- I'm sorry for what we did to you," I say, bowing my head even more. It shouldn't have happened like that, it's true.

- Get up," Alma orders, "you're not in Japan anymore, you're in Spain. If you wanted to apologise to me, you should have done so earlier.- Alma, I'm not even asking you to accept my apology, just to hear me out. Whatever James did, he didn't do it with the intention of hurting you. He thought he was doing a good thing, but he chose the worst ways to do it and so did I.

- I don't want your excuses. You destroyed my life when I saw you, that was the last straw.

- And you think you didn't destroy mine when you came here? I asked with tears in my eyes. Every day my mother saw you and your brother, she remembered that she didn't belong here. That it was her fault when it was Dad's fault for not knowing how to keep his zip shut.

Alma had a scowl on her face. She knew the truth. My mother was mocked several times for not realising the second home our father had started. Stares rained down on us, not to mention indiscreet remarks.

She was tricked into thinking he was still single.

- Stop blaming me, I didn't make him behave like that.

- Don't you remember the day of our parents' tenth wedding anniversary? When you were 15 and you got into a fight with my mother because she wouldn't let you leave the room. We all knew you were going to run away. And you started screaming at her that she was an adulteress and that she only earned her place by going under the desk. That was even why she was still here.

Because your mother was dead.

Alma looks down, troubled by my words.

- Do you know what it did to her when her husband didn't even have the courage to refute the words of a 15-year-old girl in public? I asked, looking at her sternly.

Everyone has their reasons and wrongs for acting one way rather than another and it's time to move on. I've made mistakes, but I've been able to admit them and James had better do the same.

I stand up and dust off my clothes before looking Alma in the eye.

- I know you want revenge, and that's your choice," I say. Except that before you wanted revenge, you would have tried to find out what was behind everyone's actions.

Voices echoed from the hallway and headed our way. James enters the dining room and takes me in his arms. I let him do so before taking him to our bedroom upstairs. He sits on the bed and looks up at the ceiling.

- James, we should cut the crap," I say, smiling at him.

- When we've already come this far? he asks.

- We're doing more harm than good together. I want you to find a girl who will bring out the best in you. And that girl is not me.

- So what? We're happy together," he protests, taking my hand.

- You're going back to your old ways James. Sometimes holding on does more damage than letting go. That's what we're doing. We're destroying everyone around us.

- What are you trying to tell me?

- We better break up now before it's too late. The only things that bind us together are the mistakes we've made in the past.

- No, it's not. Mila, please. . .

- Yes, it is. We both need to move on and take responsibility. It's time to grow up.

Chapter 30

Alexia is sitting in an armchair with her son in her arms.

- Alma! she calls out when she sees me. Are you having a baby?

- Yes!" I exclaimed, taking her in my arms. And my little prince!

I take her son in my arms, kissing him all over. He bursts out laughing and kisses me on the mouth.

- Even kids are trying to steal my wife now," Gabrielo sighs as he enters the room with Cordelia in his arms.

I roll my eyes as he approaches. He kisses me on the cheek and puts his free arm around my waist.

- How old is he? I ask.

- Four, it's already been five years since I left.

Gabrielo puts Cordelia down on the floor and she shyly approaches Matheo, Alexia's son. He takes her in his arms and clumsily hugs her. I observe them completely caught up in their game.

- Is that your husband? Alex asks as he approaches me.

I nod and smile. Gabrielo greets her with a nod and sits down next to me.

- Not bad, eh?

- More than not bad, in fact. When I said you'd end up with a model, I was dead right. You owe me a meal now.

- We'll talk about it when we get your problem sorted. James's mother will be here any minute. What do you expect to get out of this meeting?

- I want my son to know his grandma and his dad. He deserves to know his father, as imperfect as he is. It's not my place to make that kind of decision for him. James didn't want a child, but his grandmother deserves to know that he is out there.

- That's a nice way of thinking about it. All that is left is to see how your mother-in-law reacts, if I may say so.

James' mother enters the room a few moments later. I greet her with a hug before asking her to sit down. Gabrielo gets up to make a phone call.

- Alexia? Serena, James' mother, asks. I haven't seen you for so long. What have you been up to?

- I've become an architect. I'm working with a company in Los Angeles.

- I'm glad to hear it. Who is this adorable little child? He reminds me of James when he was younger.

- That's good because he's her son," she replies, stroking Matheo's cheek.

- I beg your pardon? Alexia, I think I misunderstood.

- No, it's your grandson.

- That's not possible. Come on, Alexia. My son wouldn't have dared...

Alexia hands her what looks to me like a paternity test. Serena takes it and begins to read it carefully. Alexia sits down and waits for Serena's reaction, which soon comes. She collapses and I barely catch her. Alexia helps me to lay her down on the sofa.

- I'd forgotten how dramatic her fainting could be," Alexia laughs.

- I'd forgotten too. Poor woman, to learn that she became a grandmother so suddenly. I feel sorry for her.

- Personally, I pity her son. She's going to rip his head off when he wakes up.

- Too bad for him. His mother has warned him so many times. Before you do something, think of all the things that could possibly happen from it.

-She wasn't wrong when she told him that," she replies.

An employee arrives with some smelling salts so that Serena can be woken up. She quickly comes to her senses after breathing them in and stands up abruptly.

- Son, bring him in," she orders around. Now!

James soon enters the room with Mila. They both walk towards Serena with a smile. She asks Mila to come out of the room so we can talk.

- James, don't you have something to say to me? she asks, squinting her beautiful azure eyes.

- What are you trying to say," he replies with a frown.

- Trust me, young man, lies won't save you. Keep it up and I'll cut you off.

- Mum, what do you mean?

- You know what I mean. I look like a fool," she yells, getting up. My son is getting a girl pregnant, and my goddaughter at that! And he doesn't even have the courage to take responsibility for what he has done.

Serena slaps her son without delay. He tries to back down, but she grabs him by the collar and lifts him up on her stilettos. Now, that I remember, this woman was a professional boxer before she married.- James, darling... Anything but that," she said menacingly. I told you never to take me for a fool. First you break off your engagement, then you get a girl pregnant. What's next? Tell me, son, huh?

She throws James to the floor and sits back down on the sofa. Alexia looks on blankly as they wait for their conversation to end. Gabrielo sends me a message to meet him in our room as soon as the conversation is over. I reply and refocus on the scene before me.

- Alexia," Serena calls, turning to her. I apologize for what my son did to you. Please let us meet Matheo once in a while.

- There's nothing to apologize for. I came so that you could meet my son," Alexia reassures her. He deserves to know his grandparents.

- Very well, then, that problem is solved. James will pay you child support every month. I want you to live quietly with Matheo without having to worry about anything. Only work if you want to and take good care of my grandson. Thank you, Alma.

I nod as I receive her thanks. They hug each other before Matheo comes to join them. I get up to leave and see James glaring at me. I smile at him before waving.

Gabrielo is waiting for me on our bed, playing with Lia on the game console they decided to buy the day before. I lie down next to him and hug him without letting him stop playing.

- Did you want to tell me something? I asked, looking at the screen.

- Yes," he said, resting his head on my shoulder. We're supposed to go home next week. What do you want to do: stay or go?

- I want to stay a little longer, but we're going to have to go back sometime," I sighed.

- We can stay another week, I have a contract to sign in exactly two weeks. Then we'll go home with Cordelia.

- Fine, that's fine with me. By then, I hope our two friends have the nursery done, because knowing them....

- They're more likely to make a baby than anything else....

-I want a baby too! Cordelia exclaimed.

- I'm sorry, sweetheart, but that's not going to be possible right now," I announced, taking her in my arms. But we can go and have lunch with Matheo if you want.

Cordelia puts down her controller and takes my hand to go and eat. Gabrielo follows us without wasting any time. I let Cordelia go ahead of us to the kitchen.

- So how did it go?

- Well...

I finish telling him what happened and he starts to laugh.

- If my mother was that scary, I would have stayed a virgin until the wedding," he laughs. And I'd probably never have set foot in a club.

- You bet. He still managed to cause so much trouble. Not to mention the fact that his father is... Special, I'd say.

- That special? He's surprised.

- Trust me, you haven't seen anything yet.

Chapter 31

Another nightmare.

They started coming a few days ago after Alexia arrived. They are getting worse and worse. To the point where I don't want to go to sleep.

- Alma? Another nightmare? he asks, taking me in his arms. Do you want to talk about it?

- I was looking in the mirror in a room. I was wearing a wedding dress that was to die for. As I zipped it up, I realised I had put on weight. A lot of weight. Yuma walked me down the aisle and once I was facing you... .

I pause, trying to regain my composure. The images are still so clear in my mind it's disturbing. My body wrapped tight in a white dress.

- What happened next? my husband asks patiently.

- Your face twisted in disgust. You started to make comments about my looks. The mayor came to ask us if we would take each other as spouses. You said word for word: "I have no intention of ending up with such a huge woman, she'll end up crushing me". The wedding stopped and then you left and I ran away from the rest of the guests.

- That won't happen," Gabrielo says. Whether you're thin, fat, normal or whatever, remember that I love you for who you are. All of you. No matter what. I love you.

- I love you too," I say, resting my head on his chest.

- Now it's time for you to answer my question, isn't it? Why are you so obsessed with your looks?

I remain silent without knowing what to say. Just thinking about it makes me want to throw up. My whole childhood and adolescence were ruined because of this.

- I-

Knock, knock!

- Come in," said Gabrielo, covering me with the sheets.

- I heard crying coming from here," Yuma announced, poking his head in the doorway. I wanted to know if everything was okay.

- Everything's fine," I replied, my voice cracking.

- You know very well that there's no point in lying to me, Alma. What's the matter? my brother asked, turning to my husband.

- She had a nightmare," he replies.

I feel Yuma's gaze burn the back of my neck.

- If you don't want to tell him, I will," he says, sitting up.

I remain silent, praying that he will come out of the room, but he doesn't. I step out from under the sheets and face my brother who looks me straight in the eye.

- It's not what you think.

- Then what? Yuma challenges me. Don't make me think it's the baby, I'm not stupid. I know you far too well to believe it.

Gabrielo keeps me in his arms without saying anything. He deserves to know. Since he plans to spend the rest of his life with me, he should know.

- I'll tell him," I said to Yuma. I'm really going to tell him.

Yuma looks at me apprehensively before leaving the room after wishing us a good night. I play with my hands and take a deep breath. Gabrielo stares at me, a soft smile on his face.

- My mother was a prima ballerina when she met my father. She danced for a big company in Russia, where she was born, and she learned everything. I wanted to follow in her footsteps when I was younger. We lived in Russia at the time, I started doing rhythmic gymnastics.

- You were an athlete? Gabrielo exclaims with astonishment.

- You could say that. I trained four hours a day every day of the week. I started to improve until I was training eight to nine hours a day. At some point I started to gain weight. It was mostly around puberty.

"My coach told me to lose three kilos in three days. And that's what I did. I remember having a supply of water bottles in my room and Yuma came to visit me. He asked me if I was eating well and I showed him the bottles.

"That was my breakfast, lunch and dinner. All to be the best. I was told I was too fat and I lost the weight I needed. After that I started freaking out at every meal because I was terrified of gaining weight.

"I continued competing like that until I was 17. My weight was constantly monitored by the coach. An extra 300g is something you can see and feel on a gymnast's body. I had a coach who could see if I gained even 100g. And her superior even more so.

"She was often harsh with her words, so we would do anything to get even one compliment. So we had to give ourselves the means.

"We started to limit my meals. The maximum was an egg for breakfast, a small piece of boiled meat or fish and that was it. I had done my day. We even couldn't drink during training.

- You're joking," Gabrielo exclaims in shock.

- That's the sad reality," I smiled. Everything we had lost would come back with a sip of water so we were deprived of it. I pushed myself to the point of overcoming my limits.

"My body couldn't take it anymore. I had health problems and it was Yuma who realised that the damage wasn't just physical. He got me out of there and taught me how to take care of myself.I love the sport but I could never hurt myself that much again. Not mentally anyway. I'm here because Yuma saved me. I remember I couldn't even walk without being in pain."

He's my other half. Always there for me when I need him.

- So the nightmares...

- It's just my fears coming back because I know I'm going to keep gaining weight with the baby. I'm so happy that we're going to have our baby in a few months. It's just my old demons coming back.

Gabrielo holds me without saying anything. He gives me a kiss on the forehead every now and then and I start to fall asleep.

- Were you going to tell me about it? he asks calmly.

- I don't think so. Everything is fine and it's not like I'm still having problems with eating now. I'm learning to accept myself a little more every day.

He doesn't say anything and we lie back on the bed in each other's arms.

- Gabrielo?

He turns his gaze towards me.

- Are you going back to sleep?

- No, it's already seven o'clock. Why?

- I have something to show you.

- What is it? he asks, frowning as I straddle him.

I take off my nightie to show him the new underwear I bought.

- What do you think?

Gabrielo doesn't take the time to answer me and kisses me. I feel his hand play with the band of my panties and pull on them. He places kisses along my neck and down to my chest. He lifts his head and smiles at me before placing a kiss where my heart is.

- I love you," he breathes as he kisses me again.

This time he moves over me effortlessly and lays me gently on the bed.

- Cordelia! I love you," I exclaimed, taking her in my arms.

If she hadn't knocked on my door to go to lunch, I'd still be in this bed. And I refuse to spend all day in bed and get sore.

- Me too," she laughs, returning my embrace.

- Alma, we can finally go home! Amber writes as she enters the room. The wedding is officially off!

- What happened?

- I have no idea," she replies, shrugging her shoulders. I heard that Mila had left, but no one knows where. She didn't take anything with her either!

- That girl exhausts me," I sighed, getting up.

- Where are you going? Amber asked.

- To check something.

I walk quickly down the corridors before opening Mila's room. Everything is in place. I approach the bed and lift the mattress before finding a paper. This was where we used to hide our letters when we were younger.

Who would have thought she would remember?

I quickly open the letter and read the contents.

There is only one thing, a phone number and a bank card. I close the envelope and put it under my mother-in-law's door. As bad as she is, she is still a mother who worries about her daughter.

This is the last thing I can do for Mila.

Chapter 32

Screams from the living room reach my room. I feel like I recognise the voice screaming. It's so strange. Gabrielo is walking into the room and has a smile on his face.

- What's wrong? I asked, stretching.

- There's quite a scene going on downstairs. You should come and have a look," he suggested, giving me a quick kiss.

- Is it that good?

- Come and see! You won't regret it.

I follow him downstairs to find pieces of glass everywhere on the floor.

- A fool and an ingrate! That's all you are!

What's going on here? The screams only get louder, not to mention the sounds of objects hitting the walls. James' father is standing in the middle of the room with a huge pile of dishes. James runs across the room and his father throws everything he can get his hands on at him.

He runs out of dishes and James sits down on the couch without saying anything. His father grabs him by the collar before letting go and pacing around. He sighs and settles into an armchair nearby.

- Before sleeping with Alexia, you should have thought about it," his father growls. Think about the consequences of your actions before you act! James, you're already 26 for God's sake!

- I'm sorry," he murmured with his head down.

- I'm not the one you should be apologising to.

- I already apologised to Alexia when she decided to leave.

- You ruined her life!

- And who told you that? Alexia?

- She had a child at 18," James' mother exclaims as she enters the room. Do you think having a child with her was a good decision?

James' point of view

It was her choice. She wanted a child. She told me that before she even slept with me. This child was planned. The only problem is that nobody knew about it. And I'm the one who takes the blame for any misery that happens to those around me.

I'm at fault, it's true. Except that she wanted this child.

I told her I didn't want to take care of a child. Alexia was clear in her answer. She wasn't going to involve me any more than that if I wasn't ready.

- You don't know anything," I mumbled, standing up.

I meet Alma's gaze, huddled in her husband's arms. She looks at me coldly before looking away.

She has every right to hate me after what I did to her. I was wrong. I wanted to apologise in the past, but she wouldn't listen. I made a mistake. I should have walked away from Mila when I noticed my feelings for her, but I couldn't. I couldn't abandon Mila.

I couldn't abandon Mila who had sacrificed everything for me as my best friend and girlfriend. The saying "Quiet relationship, perfect relationship" is totally wrong. I knew this and I wanted to believe it.

The way people look at us makes us act right. Living in hiding is the best way to go elsewhere. Now I've destroyed everything, my relationship, my best friend, even my career. I leave the mansion before going home.

I open the wine cellar and bring several bottles with me. Some time later, I hear my mother's voice calling me before she storms into the living room.

- James, what are you doing? she shouts, pushing the wine bottles away from me.

- Leave me alone. I'm begging you, just today.

- You think after what you've done you can afford to drink like you're celebrating good news?

- And you think you can afford to berate me now? I did everything I could to keep my promise. I've opened a stable investment business, I'm bringing in money all the time and people envy you! Isn't that what you wanted?

- James, have some respect for your mother," my father threatens, banging his fist on the table.

She's right and you know it.

- Why should I apologise to anyone? You made me this way! Have you ever apologised?

- I didn't make you like this," my mother yells.

- Didn't you? You're the one who told me to get on with it and that the end justifies the means in some cases. The only thing you were looking at was the results so why did you decide to change now?

A heavy silence settles over the room, I pick up my bottle of wine before leaving the house. If it were up to me, I would have thrown myself off a bridge. The only problem is that a funeral is expensive. And I'm sure I'll be criticised for being a coward.

I've done my best to keep my head on straight, but I feel I've reached my limit. No amount of apologising will erase what I've done and it's weighing heavily on my conscience.

I'll just wait for my time to come.

My phone starts ringing in my pocket. I drink my glass of wine and pick it up. Alexa.

- What can I do for you? I asked without bothering to greet her.

- James, are you sure you don't want me to talk to your mother. She's going to want you dead for something that's not worth it," she insists for the umpteenth time.

- Alexa, stop worrying about it. I'll just add the money she mentioned on top of your child support.

- No, you don't have to do that. What you already give me is plenty. James, stop being stubborn and listen to me. You know that-

- Nothing at all, Alex.

- James!

I sigh, waiting for her to start talking again.

- Why do you always take the bad part? I know you have your faults, just like anyone else, but you also have your good sides.

- Because it's easier that way. Nobody expects anything from me.

My mother has no hope for me. My father has given up and doesn't even try to tell me anything anymore.

And to think that all this started after an argument I had in college.

- I'm going to have to go," I said to Alexia. Was there something else you wanted to tell me?

- Matheo said he wanted to see you.

- I'll come to you myself as soon as I have time," I assured her before hanging up.

Alma

It's time for the big departure.

After yesterday's circus between James and his father, it's time to go home. Cordelia is already in the car with Gabrielo getting ready to leave. I have just said a tearful goodbye to my grandmother, my brother and Alexia.

Amber and Steven have been gone for a week in New York. Home seems so far away. Gabrielo has decided to fly home on a private jet for comfort and I wouldn't say no. Staying in the same position for a while is becoming difficult and having swollen legs is bad enough. The journey is getting long, especially now that I'm five months pregnant.

I'm so excited to find out if we're having a boy or a girl. Cordelia starts to move next to me. She's been sound asleep since take-off. I stroke her hair while waiting for Gabrielo to come back with food. The jet has already been in the air for two hours and I'm getting hungry. He comes back with a snack since it's still not time to eat.

- Alma, what are we going to do with Cordelia?

- What do you mean? I asked with a frown.

- How are we going to raise her with our own children? In what way?

- Like siblings, letting them know they're not related by blood. It's probably not going to happen, but she could fall in love with one of our children. If it's mutual, I want them to know that they don't have to hide their relationship. Just that I would never leave them alone in a room past a certain age.

- That's a good idea. I hope they get on well and don't mind talking to us about their problems. We're here to help them after all," he says, kissing my cheek.

- I'm so excited to see the baby," I sighed. I just wish I could avoid the painful part of giving birth.

- Life isn't that easy," Gabrielo replied, laughing softly. It's just a matter of being patient and brave.

Gabrielo's phone rings and he answers a video call. I stay close to him and Cole appears on the screen. He waves to us along with Meavy, both of us grinning from ear to ear.

- I hope you didn't sleep together at our place," Gabrielo threatens without waiting. Especially you, Cole.

- We didn't do anything," Cole exclaims.

- At least not at your place," mutters Meavy.

- Meav', I heard you. We'll talk about this when I get there," I say, watching her squirm behind the screen.

- Anyway, we wanted to tell you," Cole continues.

- We finished the baby's room! Meavy announces. Hurry up and come in, we've finished Cordelia's and Max's too. Not to brag, but we did an amazing job.

- We're going to hurry up to come and see so stay at home," Gabrielo enthuses.

- And stay for dinner, I'll be cooking for the occasion," I added.

- Yes!" they both exclaim over the phone.

Chapter 33

Welcome home! Meavy greets me with a hug.

I return her embrace and we go inside. Cordelia can't wait to see her room. She rushes upstairs with Meavy who wastes no time in showing her his masterpiece. I follow them up the stairs at my own pace, hand in hand with Gabrielo.

Max's room is amazing. Even the front door has been redone to be more vintage in engraved wood. The decorations and the paint make you feel like you are on a cloud. Everything is in pastel colours with lots of blue and pink touches that give a feeling of sparkle. Not to mention the bed that looks like a huge hot air balloon and the cloud-like decorations hanging from the ceiling.

Cordelia's room looks like a small tower with a slide and stairs connected on both sides. There are even little stairs and decorations that look like a princess castle.

It's really impressive. It's like a very elaborate bunk bed.

The work they have done in a few weeks is incredible. I didn't think they would get it done by the time we got there. Cordelia thanks Meavy and Cole with a hug and a smooch each.

We leave her in her room to play. It's time to discover the baby's room. I am so excited! We walk down the hall to our room. I turn to Cole and Meavy who look nervous.

- We forgot to mention one little thing," Cole begins, scratching the back of his head.

- 'What's that? Gabrielo asks as he comes dangerously close to Cole. 'If you didn't mention it, you must have something to blame yourself for.

- Not necessarily. It's just that you weren't asked," my best friend explains.

- Meavy, explain yourself," I asked, seeing her look away before turning to the others. You want to know what happened on my 20th birthday?

- We redid part of the flat to make the baby's room," she explained hurriedly.

- But what else?

- The cost of the work is $300,000," Cole finishes, "which we have to pay for today.A nervous laugh escapes Gabrielo. He grabs Cole by the shoulder and forces him to look him in the eye.

- What work? he asks calmly. I thought I told you there was a room next to our bedroom. Not to do any renovations.

- Gab' listen, I'm going to make sure that-

- You're not going to make sure of anything. You know very well that money is not the problem," says Gabrielo. We'll work it out together.

Cole sighs and sulks.

- Alma, please deal with your friend," adds my husband.

- Gabrielo, why don't we go to your room before we decide anything? I suggested, sensing the heavy atmosphere.

- If that makes you happy," he growls, catching me by the waist.

- Is that okay? I ask our two best friends.

They nodded and glanced at each other before sighing.

- How much did the rest of it cost, apart from the work? I asked.

- It's really best if you see the room first," Cole advises. You can judge it more quality wise afterwards.

We walk into our room, which looks unchanged except for the huge wooden double door next to our bed. We walk through the entrance into the new room.

It is beautiful. I would expect nothing less from Meavy. All the furniture is placed to fill the room and there is plenty of room to sit. She has even added a bed so that we can sleep next to it. I walk around the room before turning to see Gabrielo's face.

He's got that businessman look on his face as he examines some new merchandise. I walk over to him and take him in my arms. He returns my embrace and kisses me briefly.

- What do you think?

- It's good," he grumbles.

- Which means we can leave them alone, doesn't it, darling? Besides, we gave them carte blanche to do whatever they wanted with the flat. They should have warned us, but we also have our share of responsibility.

- Okay. It's okay," he said, sitting down on one of the sofas. - Did you hear that? You're all forgiven.

Cole picks me up and lifts me off the floor. Gabrielo quickly takes me back into his arms.

- Thank her from afar, he advises. Touch your girlfriend since she's on your left.

- Calm down, Mr Possessive," Cole exclaims. Oh dear, love really does make your head spin.

I turn to Meavy who looks away. Oh yeah?

- So Gabrielo knows, but not me?

- Alma, she calls. Cole told him....

- I didn't say anything. I just wish I'd known from you, that's all.

- I know," she mumbles. I was going to tell you today over lunch.

I smile at her before leaving the room. It's already six o'clock and time for dinner is quickly approaching. Cordelia has accompanied me downstairs to make dinner with me. We're going to make a cheesecake and lasagna. Thanks to the help of my trainee cook, we finished faster than expected.

Gabrielo came to see how things were going in the kitchen before he went out. He has his arms around my body as I try to cook as best I can.

- You really don't want to hire a cook?

- No thanks, Gabrielo. Cooking is my pleasure and the only thing I have to do in this house. We have maids who clean, do the laundry and a butler who does the shopping. That's more than enough. You even hired a housekeeper.

- If you say so. Just remember, if you ever change your mind, we'll hire right away. I'm not going to let you wear yourself out when I can avoid it.

- Get tired? I asked, raising an eyebrow.

Gabrielo nodded his head, determined.

- What do you want me to do to get tired?

He looks around and observes Cordelia. He waves his hand at her before bending down to speak into my ear.

- I'd rather have you in a bed under me than in this kitchen.

- Gabrielo!

- What? You asked me a question and I'm answering it! Women, I swear.

- Very good, sir," I said, kissing him. Now I'd appreciate it if you'd get off my back so I can cook properly. You're getting in the way and I'd like not to cut myself today.

He releases me and sits down on the counter to help Cordelia, who can finally start making the cheesecake. I put the lasagna in the oven and go out to let Gabrielo and Lia work. Meavy is in the middle of a discussion with Cole facing each other. They look concentrated, which is strange coming from them.

- Alma, how much? asks Cole.

- How much of what?

- Just tell us a number.

- 1 000.

- Okay, then, I'll bet you $1,000 that they have a girl," Meavy says.

- And I bet they get a boy," replies her boyfriend.

- Stop betting on my offspring, both of you," I say, sitting down. There are four months to go before the birth. And we don't even know the sex of the baby.

- All the more reason to place a bet," Cole exclaims. You really don't want to know?

- No, we'd rather know later. Now, end your bets and come and eat.

The table is set and everyone starts to eat. After dinner, Meavy and Cole went home and Cordelia went to sleep. I'm finally on my warm bed waiting for my husband who is in the shower. He joins me a few minutes later and takes me in his arms to sleep.

- Alma, my mother called to say we're going to a family dinner. What do you think?

- No problem. Tell me when to go and we'll go," I reply, about to fall asleep.

- Are you sure? he asked, lifting his head from my neck.

- What's the matter? Don't you want to go?

- Not really. My aunts and cousins will be there and they're... How can I put it? Overbearing.

- I think we'll be fine. Trust me on that.

- If you say so. They think we're going to have a wedding ceremony to mark it symbolically, he laughs.

- It's just to celebrate and see our loved ones. We've already signed the papers for six months.

- That's not wrong. What about Max? he asks suddenly. Now that we've got Cordelia at home, I thought we could bring him along too.

- I agree. Might as well have them all home. I'd rather get used to having them around before I give birth so I don't feel too overwhelmed by all the things to do.

- Should we call tomorrow to pick him up?

- Absolutely!

I feel Gabrielo's hand go down my nightie. He starts to pull on the elastic of my panties and I feel the sleep leave.

- I thought we were supposed to be sleeping," I asked, watching him stare at me.

- Of course we were. Afterwards," he mumbles, placing kisses down my neck.

Chapter 34

We go into the orphanage to pick up Max. I'm nervous about seeing him again after so long. Will he still want to come with us?

- This way, the director of the orphanage says. He's waiting for you in his room.

I enter the room and see Max running after a baseball. He bends down to catch it and rolls it in our direction. After chasing the ball once more, he finally grabs it and looks up.

He smiles when he sees us and hands us the ball.

- It's a gift! he exclaims with a smile.

I crouch down beside him and grab the ball, thanking him.

- Are you ready to go home with us? I asked, smiling at him. Do you want to come?

He nods and scurries off to his bed on his short legs. Gabrielo helps me up while Max walks towards me with his little backpack. I turn to the headmaster who sighs. According to him, Max had only decided to take his favourite baseball and his round sheep toy.

He had refused to bring anything else.

Max stops in front of us and raises his arms to be carried. Gabrielo goes ahead of me and picks him up. I roll my eyes and we get out before we start walking down the street. For once, I have convinced Gabrielo not to take the car.

Cordelia is at home with Meavy and Cole. She was still asleep when we left so she might be surprised. Max is enjoying the scenery and getting excited about every little thing he sees. Gabrielo can't help but smile at Max's amazement.

He was so excited that he couldn't stop wanting to touch everything he could find. After disinfecting his hands, we arrived in front of the house. Max is still full of energy. I open the door and Gabrielo lets go of his hand to let him in.

- Max? I asked as I saw him staring at the flat without daring to enter.

He slowly puts one foot inside before grabbing my hand. I stroked his hair before heading to the kitchen. As usual, Meavy and Cole are standing around the island eating something.

The amount of food they can eat will always fascinate me. Cordelia rushes towards us and stops when she sees Max. They both silently glare at each other until Max comes forward to give Cordelia a hug.

He wraps his arms around her awkwardly and Cordelia returns his embrace before leading him into her room. We follow them as they start to play together. I sit in the desk chair in Max's room and watch him play.

- If we keep up this pace, we'll be ten in this house before you've given birth," Gabrielo points out, joining me. I've got nothing against that, but if we add a baby to this, we'll start to struggle.

- I know, I suggest we stop here for now. Even if it's just until we get used to caring about Cordelia and Max.

Gabrielo nods and turns to the children. Suddenly our family has grown from two to four people in six months. I don't feel bad about it though. I've always wanted a big family so I think I'm getting there.

Little by little, the bird is nesting.

A month and a half later

- They're coming," Rosaria exclaims, taking my hand.

Gabrielo and his father get up to leave the room.

- You two! Sit down," my mother-in-law orders, giving them a nasty look. You'd better get up and see if I am in the mood to joke with you. Especially you! They're your sisters and you don't even want them in your house.

- If they weren't so annoying, maybe I'd accept them in my house. As long as they're not," my father-in-law says, "they can stay away from my house where they won't destroy anything.

They both sit down and start to ruminate. It can't be that bad. The doorbell rings in the room. A commotion approaches the living room where we are sitting.

Four women enter the room and rush towards us. Gabrielo brings me closer to him and stops the women in front of me.

- Gabrielo! the smallest of them exclaims, kissing him on the cheek. What a pleasure to see you again!

The sound of her smack resounds in the room. I stop myself from wincing when I see the vermilion lipstick on her lips.

She moves away from him and leaves us to discover two huge lipstick stains on both of Gabrielo's cheeks. He is tense from head to toe and seems to be holding back from saying something.

- Even more so now that you're married," the taller one says, pulling at his cheeks. And to think we were changing your nappies just a while ago!

She pats him familiarly on the back and Gabrielo moves slightly. I'm surprised she managed to get him to move with his large build. He is not a pile of muscle either, but he is imposing enough that it is hard to make him move.

- Not to mention your wife! She had to be six months pregnant for you to deign to introduce her to us! writes the heavier woman, taking him in her arms and smothering him in a murderous embrace.

She releases Gabrielo who already seems to be on edge.

- What a brat! And to think that we were going to come and congratulate you much earlier," adds the only woman with pink hair. We were even planning to have a little party for the occasion.

She kisses him while talking without stopping. Gabrielo is shaken in all directions and she finishes by patting his cheek.

Gabrielo seems to be at his wit's end. He looks like he's literally going to explode since their arrival. Even more so now that they are touching him all over. He inhales and exhales deeply while squeezing my hand. Suddenly he stands up and rushes towards the exit. Before he can reach the exit, three girls appear and throw themselves into his arms.

- Alma, a little help, please," he asks, trying to free himself.

- Honey, they're your family," I say, watching him from a distance. And then it's just a show of affection. It's nothing too mean.

- Just say you're too lazy to get up.

- I'm exhausted," I said honestly, leaning back against the sofa.

The baby kept me up all night last night, and let's just say I haven't been in a very good mood since this morning. The lack of sleep is doing me anything but good. And I was hoping to get a bit more sleep this afternoon. Well, I guess I didn't.

- Welcome to the family," the smallest woman exclaims as she hugs me.

- What a beautiful young woman! the taller woman, whose name is Vita, exclaims as she touches my face.

- And so well formed," the plump woman, Berta, adds. Look at those breasts and her hips.What's wrong with these women? They really can't keep their hands to themselves, it's beyond belief!

- And that baby! He must be a sight to behold if he looks like them," the pink-haired woman giggles as she prepares to place her hands abruptly on my stomach.

Gabrielo appears in an instant near us and separates his aunt from me.

- Aunt Elisa," he begins, "you know I like you a lot, but don't throw yourself at my wife as if it was nothing. I'm really not joking. She's already six months pregnant and I'd like to avoid any trouble today, it's for all of you.

Aunt Elisa apologizes and sits down more gently next to me to touch my belly after asking my permission. All this noise is seriously starting to make me tired. Especially my husband's cousins who seem to be in ecstasy over Cordelia.

- Alma, you should go upstairs and rest for a while," my mother-in-law suggests. You look a bit pale.

I smile at her before going upstairs to a guest room and lying down. I feel like a weight has been lifted from my shoulders. The quiet feels so good. The door opens and Gabrielo looks exhausted. I take him in my arms and he lies down.

- What's up? Are you running away? I snarled, stroking his hair.

- I need to run away. My father will make it on his own one way or another. He's survived this for thirty years of marriage, I don't see why he would have a problem.

- If you say so. I'm going to sleep for a while before I eat. I'm so tired I could sleep standing up.

- Sleep tight then, I'll wake you up a bit before we have to go and eat," he says, taking me in his arms.

I thank him and finally close my eyes.

As promised, I was awakened after a three-hour nap. It's almost 7pm. We're going to eat in an hour, but I'd better be awake now. Gabrielo has led me to the terrace where his cousins are. I sit down on a random chair next to Gabrielo.

His cousins give me strange looks and start talking amongst themselves. I turn to Gabrielo, not sure how to react. He shrugs innocently and glances in their direction. Rosaria calls my husband, who leaves me alone with his cousins. Great.

I start stroking my stomach nervously. The baby kicks, which makes me smile inside.

- So, you're Gab's wife? The only blonde in the group asks.

I nod and she continues.

- How did you get him to turn his head?

- I'm sure she bumped into him or something," the one on the left guesses. Just like in the shows!

- I'm sure she did too. Maybe he bumped into her and fell for her!

I watch them construct a totally crazy scenario about how I ended up marrying their cousin.

These girls have a wild imagination. I wonder how they came up with Gabrielo doing a striptease in the middle of a bar but hey.

Speaking of him, he comes quietly behind them. He raises his eyebrows with a smile and approaches me.

- I married my wife because I liked her at first sight," he says, taking me in his arms. She didn't want me, and I saw her again later, even more beautiful than ever. That was when we finally got married, because this time she was single.

He kisses me on the cheek and gives his cousins a defiant look. They finally shut up before starting again with their conspiracy theories. Rosaria arrives a little later with my husband's aunts. I get up to help them set the table against their will. Finally we all sit down at the table to start.

- I don't know if I asked you," Rosaria begins. You must know the baby's gender, right?

- We've decided to have a surprise at the birth," I announced.

- Did we? Rosaria insisted. I wanted to have a baby shower.

- Next time," Gabrielo replied.

- That means there will be another baby," Rosaria concluded in satisfaction. Good, I'll do the baby shower later.

- And the wedding," Aunt Elisa asks. When will the ceremony take place? I wanted to eat cake.

- Probably when the baby is old enough to walk," I replied, glancing at Gabrielo.

- That's a very good idea, I don't want to get married between two baby bottles or two nappies," he agreed.

Chapter 35

I never thought I'd say this, but I want to give birth. I've got three weeks to go before I'm due and let me tell you, between boredom, my working husband and friends who spend their lives partying I'm starting to want my freedom again. Or an occupation at least.

In this state, Gabrielo refuses to let me go out, even if it's just to go to the shop, for fear that my water will break there. I tried to reassure him, but nothing helped. So I've officially been cooped up at home for a week and a half. And it's very boring.

Despite the presence of Cordelia and Max, who add a bit of spice to my day, the hours that pass seem to be endless after a while.

I can't even go down the street to buy bread and have to call the housekeeper to go and do it. Cole and Meavy come by every other day to keep me company until Gabrielo gets back from work. Everything seems to be going well between them for the moment.

- Hi," Gabrielo says, giving me a kiss.

- How was your day?

- The usual routine. How about you?

- Seriously? I asked as he nodded. Apart from going to the toilet, sleeping and eating, nothing. You don't want to let me out?

- No," he answered flatly.

- I've got over three weeks to go before I'm full term. And staying inside all day is bad for my health. Ask Cole if you don't believe me.

- I'm sure you're exaggerating," he replies, sitting down at the other end of the bed.

- We'll see.

A few hours later, Meavy came to see me and Cole. Gabrielo came to ask him if staying at home was bad for your health. To which Cole replied:

- Staying inside the house 24 hours a day will increase her anxiety level. She's likely to have problems with appetite, mood and sleep. It even increases the risk of health problems, he concluded.

- I was right," I scoffed as he sighed. So what do you think?

- You can go out, but let me know and don't go out alone.

- Thank you, sir," I said, giving him a kiss on the cheek before jumping up and down with Meavy.

The children are already asleep and we all had dinner an hour ago. We have the evening to ourselves without being able to go out, of course.

Meavy pats my hand and we continue our conversation. We will be able to start our Fridays together again as usual. Now it's time to tell them. Or not. I feel like the contractions I've had since earlier are not going away. They last longer and longer and make it hard for me to concentrate.

The pain radiates to my lower back and I feel as if something is pressing on my pelvis. Another contraction comes up and takes me by surprise.

- Alma, are you okay? Meavy asks with a worried look on her face.

- I'm fine. Just contractions, it'll pass," I say as I lie on the couch with my head on her thighs.

She strokes my hair and I lie as comfortably as possible. Gabrielo gives me a worried look, but I reassure him that everything is fine. After an hour, I start to think that I might actually give birth. The pain of the contractions is getting worse and worse and they are getting closer and closer.

I stand up to walk around and see if the contractions will pass. I feel a warm liquid gush out and run down my legs. I look down and see a puddle.

- Gabrielo? I say as best I can under the contractions.

- What's wrong? he asks, turning to me.

- I think my water has broken.

- Did it?

He quickly gets up to join me and sits me down on one of the chairs. Meavy goes upstairs to get the bag prepared for the delivery while Gabrielo carries me to the car. We arrive at the hospital quickly before being taken care of.

I'm currently on a bed hearing that a doctor is coming to give me an epidural. I feel like I'm going to lose my mind from the intensity of the contractions. Gabrielo takes me in his arms to comfort me.

- I can't take it anymore," I breathed deeply. It feels like it's never going to stop.

I stop myself from screaming when the doctor finally enters the room. He comes in with a huge needle and I start to rethink my choice. I'll probably be fine without it. I'm sure I can handle the pain. He approaches and another contraction hits me.

I refuse the epidural and Gabrielo gives me a worried look.

- Are you sure about this? he asks. The injection will make you feel better.

- If you want to get an injection, go ahead," I growl, "I won't stop you. But I don't want him to inject me with a needle that long.

A midwife talks to the doctor before coming over to us.

- Your cervix is already open to almost 9 cm. We'll wait a little longer and then you can go into the labour ward.

The contractions intensify and I begin to regret my decision. Tears well up in my eyes from the pain. I take a deep breath and try to focus on something else. I'll have my baby in a few hours and it will all be worth it.

- How are you feeling? Gabrielo asks, stroking my cheek with his thumb.

- Like I should have stayed a virgin a little longer.

- Poor thing," Gabrielo laughs. Believe me, this pain will soon be forgotten when the baby is born.

- Believe me, I want to turn around and take the epidural," I said through clenched teeth.

- Are you sure? That needle looked really long to me.

- Gabrielo, shut up," I growled with my eyes closed as another contraction came on. I'm going to ask the doctor to stick you with this damn needle if you mess with me.

- Stellina, you're in far too much pain for that," he laughed.

- It's funny, isn't it?

Gabrielo nods, smiling.

A moan of pain escapes me.

- What's ironic is that this is how we got here," he laughs, looking at me.

- Laugh, laugh, we'll see if it happens again.

Gabrielo becomes silent. He takes my hand before giving me puppy dog eyes.

After an hour and a half, I am finally taken to the delivery room. The contractions are even stronger. Gabrielo enters the room with me and the gynaecologist and midwives arrive. She puts an instrument on my belly and listens. She frowns and asks one of the midwives to get a cardiologist.

- What's going on, doctor? I asked nervously.

- No, we're just going to do a routine check-up to see if everything is okay," she replies, smiling warmly.

I continue to breathe deeply as a midwife asks the doctor if everything is okay.

- I hear a noise that worries me, that's all," she replies gently. I want to make sure everything is okay.

Gabrielo gently squeezes my hand and puts kisses on it.

- It's okay, honey. Everything is fine," he says calmly. We'll see the baby in a few moments and you can see which of our two best friends won the bet they made.

- Did you hear them? I asked with a smile that was soon replaced by a grimace.

- Of course I did. They even upped the winnings to a grand.

I laughed before letting out a scream as the contractions became unbearable. Gabrielo continues to reassure me and turns to the doctor who is finishing his discussion with the cardiologist they have brought in.

- There's still a long time to go before we can start, I ask.

At this rate, I'd rather he cut open my stomach to put me out of my misery.

- Why is it taking so long? My husband says, irritated.

- It's all right," the doctor replies. I thought we had a little problem, but everything is fine. Let's get started. Alma, how are you feeling?

- Fine," I huffed, wincing.

- Good, good. I heard you refused the epidural. You'll feel the reflex to push, follow your instincts," the doctor advised gently. It's now. Now, go ahead. Push!

I start to push and watch the hands of the clock tick down. Two hours have already passed and I am exhausted. I give a big push and hear crying echoing in the room.

- This is it. The doctor says and shows me my baby.

I burst into tears of relief and Gabrielo embraces me. The midwife hands me my baby and I take him in my arms.

- Let me introduce you to your little boy," she says with a smile.

- He's adorable," I say, holding him gently against me. And he already has his father's eyes, blue as the ocean.

- I'm sorry," the midwife said apologetically as she reached for the baby. You will see him again in a short while. I'll get him back to you as soon as I can.

Not now. I sigh before leaving my child in the midwife's care. Gabrielo shakes my hand with an encouraging smile.

- Ouch! I shouted as I felt a second wave of contraction coming.

- I knew it! the doctor exclaimed with a smile.

- What's the matter? Gabrielo asks nervously.

- The labour is not over," the doctor states as more contractions come.

I push again before lying back on the bed.

- That's what I thought," she continues.

- I thought so," she continues.

-"What? Gabrielo insists. What's going on?

- They're twins and the second one is coming. It's a rare phenomenon, but it can happen. The second one has hidden behind the first.

- I'm tired. Gabrielo, I can't go on, I begged.

- Come on, Alma, my husband encourages me by shaking my hand. It's almost over, just one more time.

- Push as soon as you feel it, the doctor adds.

The delivery process continues and I push a few more times before finally waiting for my baby to cry. Finally. I fall back on the bed, feeling sleep come over me.

- And here's a pretty little girl, the doctor announces.

I hold the child in my arms as the tears come to my eyes again. It is over. I finally have peace. No more pain, no more contractions. Just a few hours of sleep to lose in the future.

- Thank you Gabrielo. Thank you from the bottom of my heart," I said, unable to stop smiling.

- Thank you," Gabrielo said, kissing my forehead. This is the happiest day of my life, Alma. I'm so happy I want to cry.

I wipe away a tear that escapes his eyes and put my arms around him again.

I hug him as best I can and he kisses me.

- I swear I will do everything in my power to make you all happy," he says, putting his lips to my forehead.

Chapter 36

I wake up to the sunlight. Gabrielo is next to me and hugs me. The children are being brought into the room by one of the midwives. I thank her as quietly as possible and she smiles at me.

- Hey," I say as my husband wakes up.

- You were told not to speak yesterday," he reminds me, running his thumb over my lips.

- They brought the children back," I whispered, nodding to him. Look.

Gabrielo turns and looks at the two children by the bed. He hands me our son first before taking our daughter. Who would have thought this day would come so soon? I still remember our wedding day, our honeymoon and our time in Spain. I feel like I've stepped forward in time.

I put the children down to wash and dress. I get up all sore and go to wash up. I come out all clean and Gabrielo does the same. I watch my children on their beds. Gabrielo comes out of the bathroom and sits on the bed.

- What's up? he asks. How does our new mum feel?

- Full of love and joy. And the new dad?

- I'm so happy I feel like I'm going to explode," he laughs, holding me close.

He places a kiss on my shoulder and stares at the children. We look into each other's eyes before smiling a little more. I hold Gabrielo against me and he kisses my forehead.

The doctor knocks before entering the room. He approaches the beds and smiles at the children.

- It's about time you fed your babies," she says, approaching the beds.

- But they are still sleeping," I pleaded, looking at them. You can let them sleep a little longer.

- They will lose weight if you let them sleep too much without eating. They need to eat every three to four hours, that's crucial," the doctor said. Between 5 and 6 weeks, they will be a bit older and their sleep will be more organised so they will probably wake up to eat on their own.

- They still need to nap in the afternoon," says Gabrielo.

- It's essential for their growth. It's best if they sleep every five hours or so," advises the paediatrician. You'll see in a month how they'll be.

She rolls the children's bed over to me.

- Go ahead and hold them. Are you going to breastfeed or bottle-feed them?

- Breastfeed them," I answered confidently.

She hands me my daughter first. Gabrielo accompanies her outside while I nurse my children. I position her and she starts to latch on. It hurts a little more than I expected. It's a peculiar sensation but I think I can handle it.

A huge smile comes over my face. I can't help it. My child is finally in my arms, eating. I finish nursing them both and Gabrielo enters the room.

We sit down on the bed and the children are already sleeping. Someone knocks on the door and Rosaria enters the room. She hugs me and congratulates me.

- What a wonderful surprise, Alma! she exclaims with a beaming smile.

- Keep it down, Rosa," her husband says. You'll wake up the children.

He sighs before turning to me.

- Congratulations, darling," he says, giving me a hug.

I sit comfortably on the bed watching my in-laws rave about my children. Gabrielo hugs me and I snuggle up to him.

- Don't you think it's a bit dark in here? My mother-in-law asks as we nod.

She opens the curtains covering the huge window in front of the bed we are in. All the faces of our loved ones are revealed before us. It brings tears to my eyes to see them all here, present for the occasion. Even my grandmother and my brother are present. Amber, Steven, Meavy, Cole, Alexia, Cordelia, Max, Matheo, Christian and Jayna. They are standing there smiling with bouquets of flowers and gifts.

Everyone enters the room at the same time and I hug them all one after the other. They all turn to look at the children with a few exceptions.

- Chiquita, how are you? Yuma asks, tousling my hair as usual.

- I feel like I'm on cloud nine. What more could I ask for?

- Right, what more could I ask for," my brother repeats, lying down on the bed as if nothing had happened.

- Get yourself a wife before you say that," I retorted, forcing him to sit down.

- Always talking about marriage," he complained. Take care of my nephews and leave my bachelorhood alone.

I laughed at his words and he got up to see the children. Since everything is fine, we can go home later. Gabrielo has already gone to sign the papers for us to go out. It's going to be a restful ride home.

At least that's what I thought until everyone came home with us to celebrate the arrival of the twins. Everything was set up with balloons and decorations everywhere. We had a photo taken all together for the occasion. All the family and friends arrived afterwards. Gabrielo's aunts arrived with their noise and their children as chatty as ever this time.

Meavy approaches me and takes me in her arms. We are finally in a quiet place away from all the noise with the children.

- So what are you going to call them? my best friend asks impatiently.

- You'll know when everyone else does," I replied, raising my eyebrows.

- Alma, I am your friend! Tell me first," she demands.

- No way. I promised Gabrielo that we would announce it together. We even ordered a huge cake for the occasion. It must have arrived already. So, what about your bet with Cole?

- We changed the terms when we found out they were twins. We decided to bet on the child who was born first. I bet on your son and he bet on your daughter.

- Ah. So I guess he owes you money, right?

- Not at all," denies Meavy. He owes me a wedding with a wedding dress personally made by you.

- Are you getting ahead of yourself or is it already that serious between you?

- This is the first time I've liked someone so much and it seems to be mutual. He's meeting my parents next month and I've already met his.

We continue our conversation until Rosaria comes to pick us up, as the cake has just arrived. We join the rest of the people with the children. They are sleeping so peacefully, I envy them.

Gabrielo takes my hand and we both walk forward in front of all our guests. Gabrielo asks for their attention before he starts talking.

- As you all know, or rather you don't know, the names of the twins. We are going to announce them to you today.

He takes our son in his arms and smiles at him.

- This is Iyan (eye-an) Alessio Moretti," he proudly announces, giving our son a kiss.

This time I take our daughter in my arms. My gaze fixes on my maternal grandmother. I smile at her and she smiles back.

- This is Isla (eye-la) Olivia Moretti.

I see my grandmother burst into tears. I go up to her and she hugs her great-granddaughter.

- Thank you, Alma. With all my heart. Giving your mother's name was the best gift you could have given me.

- She reminds me a lot of her with her big blue eyes like the ocean and her little nose. I hope she will be as beautiful as her grandmother," I said, giving my grandmother a hug.

You have to know that Grandma turned some heads in her time. She was a Colombian who was simply divine. I wish I could be more like her, but you can't have everything in life.

Yuma takes Isla from my arms and walks over to a couch where he starts to watch her. He takes a picture before taking my son from the arms of my frowning husband. He starts his photo shoot and I roll my eyes. Just born and my children are already models. I had forgotten that Yuma's profession and great passion was photography.

In fact, Gabrielo hired him during our stay in Spain after seeing some of his pictures. They are now going to be in partnership since my brother already has his own photo studio. It looks like business is going very well on their side.

- Everyone get into position," Yuma writes with my children in his arms. We're going to take a big picture since you weren't all in the one before.

Last Chapter

Two years and three months later

- Iyan, Isla, come back here," Rosaria calls out from the courtyard. It's your parents' wedding, behave yourselves! Cordelia! Take a hint from Max and stop running!

A laugh escapes me from the room where I am getting ready. These kids are always so lively. And there's not one of them to outrun the other. I sigh as the hairdresser finishes doing my hair. My make-up is already done and all I have to do is put on my dress.

- Alma," Meavy says as she walks into the room. You look stunning! And that dress fits you perfectly! I can't believe you're getting married.

- You realise I've been married for three years now. I waited until it was the exact same day to celebrate. I'm the one who can't believe you got married. And that you are pregnant on top of it!

- I already told you that it wasn't really planned. But it's a very nice surprise," she smiled, stroking her already showing belly.

It's true that she's already four months pregnant. The time has gone by so quickly. I can't believe it. We're getting married in front of the mayor, because I found out that our wedding had a slight witness problem for my part. Everyone is supposed to be there today.

- 'Relax,' said Meavy, turning to the mirror. "You're the most beautiful bride I've ever seen. Your husband loves you to death and I saw the proof when I saw the huge fountains of chocolate, wine and champagne on the way here. Your princess wedding is happening."

- I know," I said with a lump in my throat. "I'm just so happy that I'm afraid it's all going to end. We're even changing our wedding rings for the occasion, I can't believe it."

- They'll be customized this time," Meavy replies. Come on, get up! Let's go to the women's room so they can see you.

We leave the room and go to the next room where my mother-in-law, my grandmother, my husband's aunts and mine are. I have reconnected with my maternal family and we are getting along very well. Everyone is chatting and stops when I arrive.

I receive compliments from everyone and thank them with a hug. Yuma comes into the room and gives me a hug. Everyone leaves the room to leave us.

- I can't believe I'm going to walk you all the way down the aisle," he whispers in a broken voice.

- Don't cry," I ordered with a lump in my throat. I'm not going to cry now, even though I'm wearing waterproof make-up. We'd better sit down for a while.

- I brought my girlfriend with me today," my brother announced.

- Seriously? Show me a picture, I want to see it.

- You'll see her later when we eat," he answers mysteriously. More seriously, I'm proud of what you turned out to be. A beautiful young woman, mother and a fabulous designer. All you have to do is learn how to clean the toilet and you're done.

- I'm gonna put your head in the toilet, you idiot.

- The limo's waiting for us downstairs. Let's go. Your husband was about to walk here from the reception," he laughs.

I smile as I stand up. We go downstairs and get into the limousine. The children get in with us and we drive off. Isla comes over and gives me a kiss.

- Pretty mommy," she says, hugging me with her little arms.

- The prettiest," Iyan adds, giving me a hug too.

- You too, my darlings. Cordelia, come here. Max too!

I hug them with the twins. Since they were born, Cordelia has been much more reluctant to come to us. She has her place in our family just like any of my children. They already share everything together so they can afford to share me.

Max for his part is always so calm and composed. I hope he stays that way as time goes by. Meavy assures me that he will become a real troublemaker, which I strongly fear.

- Happy wedding, Alma," she whispers in my ear.

- Thank you so much, Lia. You look lovely today. You all are.

- What about me? Yuma takes offense.

- I can't believe it. You're jealous of the children!

- Not at all! It's just that you compliment them much more than they deserve. I deserve compliments! I put on a shirt for the first time in five years!

- At least they're cute.

I laugh and the limo pulls up. Yuma gets out and helps the kids out first. He helps me down and leads me inside.

- I'm stressing.

- All the best, chiquita," he murmurs before taking his place as best man.

The mayor begins his speech. Silence falls over the room.

- Alma Sofia Pearson, do you take Gabrielo Leandro Moretti as your husband, to love him as you did on the first day, for richer or for poorer, in sickness and in health, till death do you part?

- I do," I said with a big smile.

- Gabrielo Leandro Moretti, do you take Alma Sofia Pearson as your wife," the mayor began before being cut off by Gabrielo.

- I do," he says before kissing my hand.

- Well, I officially pronounce you husband and wife. Let's proceed to the exchange of rings.

We turn to Isla and Iyan who are coming towards us as fast as they can. Iyan walks towards his father and Isla towards me. They each hand us our rings which we put on. The twins hug and smile at each other.

We turn to our guests who start to applaud. We walk out of the town hall and into the reception hall. Cordelia leads the way and throws petals in front of us. We get into the limousine and it takes us to the reception hall to eat and dance.

- Let's cut the wedding short and get straight to the part I'm most interested in: the wedding night," Gabrielo whispers in my ear.

- Gabrielo," I say, slapping his shoulder. This is our wedding. We're not going to stand everyone up.

- I don't mind. We'll let the kids do the show and we'll slip away. They're more than capable. Look at Cordelia posing like a model with Max. And Isla pretending to be a singer with Iyan dancing.

- No way. We'll go celebrate and I'll have fun with you tonight," I whispered in her ear.

We arrive at the hall and everyone sits down to eat. I finally get to meet my brother's lover. Speaking of him, here he comes with a small brunette with curly hair. She has a huge smile on her face and looks at him with shining eyes. We chat while we eat. It's time to dance.

Gabrielo takes my hand and we do the moves we have been practising for the last two months. We kiss at the end and the guests ask to hear our wedding vows. I let Gabrielo begin.

- Today I take you, Alma, to be my wife as you are. I promise to love, respect and cherish you now and forever. We already have four beautiful children of whom I am proud. Thank you, for choosing me and marrying me. I love you," he says, kissing me.

I wipe a tear from my eye and take Gabrielo's hand.

- Gabrielo, you have given me love, beautiful children and a family. By loving what I know of you and trusting what I don't yet know, I give you my hand. I give you my love. I give you myself, the good, the bad, and especially the future.

The guests applaud and we hug. The children come towards us to do the surprise we had planned for today. Iyan hops up to grab a microphone which Cordelia passes to him. They look at each other before turning to us.

- Gabrielo, we have a surprise," Cordelia exclaims with a big smile through the microphone.

- What do you have for me, sweatheart?

- A little brother! The four children exclaim, jumping up and down among themselves.

Gabrielo turns to me with a frown. His gaze moves from my face to my stomach before he picks me up and lifts me off the ground.

- Surprise," I say, shaking my hands.

- I'm going to be a dad again! he laughs as he spins me around.

I laugh as I let him do it and he puts me back on the ground. There is a lot of applause around us and our relatives come to join us. They hug us and the party begins.

The End

CPSIA information can be obtained
at www.ICGtesting.com
Printed in the USA
LVHW012246291122
734192LV00013B/520

9 781837 611768